Woman, Why Are You Weeping?

Woman, Why Are You Weeping?

Daily Meditations for Lent

John Timmerman

Liguori

LIGUORI, MISSOURI

Imprimi Potest: Thomas D. Picton, C.Ss.R.
Provincial, Denver Province • The Redemptorists

Published by Liguori Publications • Liguori, Missouri
www.liguori.org

Library of Congress Cataloging-in-Publication Data

Timmerman, John.
    Woman, why are you weeping? : daily meditations for Lent / John Timmerman.
        p. cm.
ISBN-13: 978-0-7648-1560-7
        1. Jesus Christ—Name—Meditations. 2. Lent—Meditations. 3. Catholic Church—Prayer-books and devotions—English. I. Title.
BT590.N2T57 2007
242'.34—dc22   2006030818

The excerpt from the song *If That Isn't Love* (page 9) by Dottie Rambo, copyright 1969. All rights reserved. Used with permission of Brentwood-Benson Publishing, 741 Cool Springs Blvd., Franklin, TN 37067.

The excerpt from "Carrion Comfort" (page 18) from *Poems of Gerard Manley Hopkins*, edited by Gardner, W. H., MacKenzie, N.H. (1970). Used with permission of Oxford University Press on behalf of the British Province of the Society of Jesus.

Unless otherwise noted, Scripture citations are taken from the *New International Version*, copyright 1978 by Zondervan Bible Publishers, Grand Rapids, Michigan. All rights reserved. Used with permission.

Liguori Publications, a nonprofit corporation, is an apostolate of the Redemptorists. To learn more about the Redemptorists, visit *Redemptorists.com.*

Printed in the United States of America
11 10 09 08 07   5 4 3 2 1
First edition

For Pat,
With gratitude to God
for our many years together.

CONTENTS

INTRODUCTION

What We Can Know

When I study the gospels, Jesus' life appears as a series of rapid-fire glimpses. In our own time, biographies of famous people frequently approach a thousand pages. Every little detail is gleaned from the historical past, dusted off, and pasted together to form a fuller picture. Too often, when I read such works, I find myself wondering, "Who cares?"

With Jesus I care passionately. There is so much I would like to know. I would like detailed pictures of Bethlehem on that ragged night when Mary gave birth. Were the nearby cattle startled by her motherly cries during labor? Did Joseph have any idea how to gentle the birth with his rough carpenter's hands? How very much I'd like a detailed account of Jesus' temptation in the wilderness. What did Satan look like? We have no documentary photographs, only a few brief words saying it happened. And so, too, no matter how fearful, I wonder what it was like—in detail—on Calvary when Jesus died. I want to watch—from the fringes, hidden by some scrub brush—while the earth shakes and the nails pound. But the dust would be in my eyes, and I'd have to turn my head with tears running down my face. I would wonder how those brave women could stay there—at the foot of the cross.

We do not have a video documentary of Jesus, and we do not have a multivolume biography of this person who, nonetheless, remains the one person most frequently written *about* in all history. The reason is simple.

At the close of his Gospel, John confesses the inability of merely human words to contain the majesty and mystery of Jesus' life: "Jesus did many other things as well. If every one of them were written down, I suppose that even the whole world would not have room for the books that would be written" (21:25). But we are also mindful of John's comment shortly before that: "[T]hese are written that you may believe that Jesus is the Christ, the Son of God, and that by believing you may have life in his name" (20:31).

The Bible, as one saying has it, contains all that we need to know and all that we are able to know about God. The Bible is not a "five-step" manual to solve all life's problems; it is a one-step guide to eternal life. But it does not leave us wandering in a directionless maze, seeking some kind of cosmic karma. God has revealed himself with blue-skied clarity, the light of his glory falling upon us in countless ways.

His clear directions for Christian living appear in both Testaments as a means for walking closely in love with God. Unless we draw close to someone, we will never get to know him or her well. God knows this. Another way God reveals himself, however, appears in the many familiar, domesticated names and titles the Bible gives to Jesus. These names—The Good Shepherd, The Bread of Life, and such—reveal Jesus to us in terms of our limited human understanding. If we can never fathom the mystery of God becoming human to save humanity, we can begin to fathom that love by comparing it to the Good Shepherd who seeks out the lost sheep and lays down his life for his flock. Or to the bread that sustains our life. Or the water without which our life is as parched as a desert.

I particularly need help from these familiar names when I come to the season of Lent, the time of Jesus' betrayal, crucifixion, and resurrection. Couldn't God have found some other miracle to permit us salvation? Why the horror of allowing his Son to die? But, on the other hand, what was it like to crush Satan's head at the crucifixion—as God had promised already in Genesis 3:15? What happened in that glory-blast of light in the resurrection? The mystery is too huge for my mind to take the plunge. Like hang-gliding through the Grand Canyon, too many turns and twists lurk to send my mind plummeting. I need solid ground, familiar terrain. Graciously, God has provided that.

My aim in this devotional study, then, is quite simple. As we approach the Lenten season, I invite you to walk with me over that ground God has provided to know him and his Son. The journey is not terribly long—only forty meditations. But then, the life of our Lord on this earth was not terribly long either. Less than forty years. Our direction in these devotions winds through some of the familiar—and some not so familiar—names and titles of Jesus that give us special insight into the passion, the crucifixion, and the resurrection of our Lord.

THE FAITHFUL AND TRUE

W hat do we prize above all things in our human relationships?

When I was examining a short story in an American Literature course once, I paused in the flow of discussion. I sensed that we were discussing the story like some disembodied fairy tale, something that could not possibly be true. It was, basically, a love story: one young woman's longing for an ideal love, only to find reality constantly intruding on it. It was a love story of loneliness and loss. Certainly I want the students to tackle a literary work in intellectual ways, but I also want them to embrace it with the heart.

So I stopped the discussion. "Without pausing to deliberate," I said, "write down the top three qualities you look for in a future spouse." As the comments quickly started to flow, I began to list them on the board. Many were typical. A good provider. A sense of humor. Open with emotions. Friendship. The list went on. But beyond question, the most highly valued quality, appearing repeatedly, was faithfulness. I don't think a single person had left it off their individual lists.

I think those students recognize that we live in a time when promises of fidelity snap as easily as a twig. They also don't want it to happen to them. They want to avoid the pain and loneliness, to be sure, but they also want to have someone on whom they can depend, who will not change, who will be there for them in their time of need.

We value faithfulness, not as a puppy-dog slavishness, but as a deeply committed devotion. I will be there for you. For better or worse. For richer or poorer. In sickness and in health. These are the treasures we long for, the ones that make our lives rich beyond compare, no matter what our circumstances.

Precisely at this point, Jesus reaches into the most profound mystery of our spiritual and psychological nature. Our human relationships, even the best intentioned of them, have a tragic way of breaking down. It is so very hard to be faithful and true to all that we wish to be. Saint Paul had no more success than any of us: "For what I do is not the good I want to do; no, the evil I do not want to do—this I keep on doing" (Romans 7:19). I can read the testament of my own life in those lines.

Fidelity is also one of the most highly valued qualities in Scripture. From its earliest accounts (Adam and Eve in Eden) through the latest directives to the Church, fidelity is the value that leads to blessing; infidelity causes destruction and loss of relationships. Threading through every single one of those situations, however, is the granite-like assertion that our God—who never changes—is faithful and true.

Deuteronomy 32:4 testifies that "He is the Rock, his works are perfect, / and all his ways are just. / A faithful God who does no wrong, / upright and just is he." In a world strewn with broken faithfulness, how can we begin to comprehend that? David, who knew well the results of infidelity, similarly testifies to God's unfaltering faithfulness. With a powerful fervor, that flawed warrior of Christ, Saint Paul, states that "Jesus Christ our Lord…is faithful" (1 Corinthians 1:9). In Jesus, we find our true home where we dwell in faithfulness.

In the Book of Revelation, Jesus appears as a rider on a white horse (signifying purity) and is called "Faithful and True" (19:11). At the close of this study, we will return again to that powerful name. That is where our Lenten passion leads—to the victorious rider called Faithful and True.

But that powerful image of the rider must also appear at the start. Isaiah prophesied "a man of sorrows, and familiar with suffering" (53:3). Can this be the same victorious rider of Revelation? In a sense, Jesus earned the "right" to be called the Faithful and True. His journey was one of suffering. The glory of Lent lies in the victorious rider; the reality of Lent also lies in the "one from whom men hide their faces" (53:3).

As we engage the names of Jesus that help us better understand him as our Lord, our friend, and our Savior, we remember that we get to know him through suffering, but we rejoice with him through victory. All this hinges on a name and a promise: he is the Faithful and True.

2 Thessalonians 3:3

But the Lord is faithful, and he will strengthen and protect you from the evil one.

Prayer

Lord, here at the very outset,
when I come looking for calm and peace,
wanting to set my heart on your heart,
placing my will in your will,
please strengthen me on the journey.
Keep me, Lord, faithful and true.
Amen.

THE CARPENTER:
THE PERSON AND THE PROFESSION

The park across the street from where we then lived was a magic summertime kingdom for children. It was not an elaborate amusement part, to be sure. A basketball court backed against the school, sided by one sagging and cracked tennis court. The play area held a large sandbox dirtied with twigs and rocks that helped to form the children's projects, from sandcastles to road systems. Off to one side resided monkey bars of dubious quality, and a dozen swings that squealed louder than the children who rode them. A good-sized wading pool was filled with seemingly equal parts water, chlorine, and small bodies. Around its edges parents relaxed in the sun and kept an eye on the bustling little bodies.

One little red-haired boy wandered from one group to another. He stood before a dozing parent and insistently hollered, "Hi." The salutation, designed to snap open the eyelids and gain attention, was followed by two questions: "What's your name?" and "What do you do?"

Whether he knew it or not, this little red-haired dynamo was a remarkable reflection of society with his two questions. We too tend to identify people with their occupations. Who I am becomes allied with what I do. "I am a teacher"—immediately certain mental pictures and a number of associations arise about who I am.

In modern society this identification becomes both a good thing and a bad thing. How is it good? Many of us feel a calling from God to pursue a certain profession or occupation. The person called to be a homemaker, who takes pleasure and satisfaction from the complex tasks of that hard work, may feel deep satisfaction by being identified as "homemaker." The person who feels called to be an editor, who has been given gifts for writing and guiding the writing of others, similarly may feel great pleasure by being identified as "editor." If Christians feel they are given certain gifts by God, and are thereby "called" to use those gifts in a certain way, it is a very good thing to be identified according to the profession in which those gifts are exercised, regardless of the profession. The *who* we are is identified with the *what* we do.

However, our society often stereotypes certain occupations. The public perceives that it seems more noble to do one kind of work than another, implying that one worker is a better person than another simply because of profession. For some reason, society sees the work of teaching, for example, as more noble than that of a mechanic; the work of a doctor as more noble than teaching. I find this a tragic and sinful attitude. The Bible teaches us the nobility of the *person*—redeemed by Jesus, not by profession.

More than once my own family has talked about this at the dinner table. It would start with a comment like this from my then eight-year-old, "I want to run a candy store when I grow up." Great! Or the thirteen-year-old says, "I think I'll be a doctor or a lawyer." The baby is busy shoveling in dessert, maybe thinking, "I'd like to be stuffed with ice cream." Years later, I now see that each of the comments was more a reflection of how the children saw themselves, perhaps, than a realistic appraisal of what they would someday do for an occupation. At such times, however, we also talked about Jesus having a plan for each of us. We talked about his plan for us to be a family, to be his children. We talked about money, which also, by today's twisted standards, seems to bestow dignity and worth upon a profession. "Our Father," Pat reminded us, "owns the cattle on a thousand hills. He's king of heaven and earth." There's the big picture we can't lose sight of.

As in every area of life, Jesus provides us a pattern that corrects our own course.

Jesus entered this life as the *Messiah*, the Lord of lords, the King of kings. A familiar church song says, "He left the splendor of heaven." For what? For a filthy stable as a birthplace, for starters. For his calling as

God's son to be our Savior, a calling that led him straight, unwavering, and relentlessly to the cross. But also to work.

Suppose that little red-haired boy in the park stormed up to Jesus one summer day. "Hi," he shouts. "What's your name?"

"Jesus."

"What do you do?"

"I'm a carpenter."

The King as carpenter—here is the fascinating, human nature of Jesus. In our own professions, our own daily work, we do well to remember the name and nature of Jesus as—the Carpenter. It reveals much about who he is and his calling on this earth.

2 Chronicles 2:4–5

> "Now I am about to build a temple for the Name of the LORD my God and to dedicate it to him....The temple I am going to build will be great, because our God is greater than all other gods."

Prayer

> Jesus, day by day, I too am building
> the house of God. In my family,
> in my work, in my play,
> may I be faithful to that great plan
> you have given, to establish the house of God
> in time and for eternity.
> *Amen.*

Day Three

THE CARPENTER: HUMAN CRAFTSMAN

E xcept for occasional sermons on the Sunday preceding Labor Day, usually a day on which we are thinking about anything *but* work, we seldom hear about the dignity and calling of work.

When God created Eden, he could have created it as a playground. In a sense he did. Eden was a place of creation and for recreation. The tour guide was the Lord himself when he came to talk with Adam and Eve. Here, working "by the sweat of the brow" was not yet known. Eden was a place among gardens, the garden of the world, suited for the most high King.

The creation of the garden itself, however, was certainly work, from which God rested on the seventh day. Moreover, it was a place for work. By making it such, God bestowed dignity and responsibility upon Adam and Eve. Thereby work also acquires dignity, and therefore brings us into relation with God. A major theme of the early Church was that in spiritual and human affairs we are all equal. Before God, a shoemaker stands as noble as an emperor. Both are sinful; both may be redeemed to eternal life. Both are required to do their daily work conscientiously in the spirit of the Redeemer.

What was that spirit? Jesus could have selected any profession he wished. He was, after all, the Messiah, the anointed one. He was, by his essential nature, the ruler of heaven and earth. But for work, he became a carpenter. By doing so, Jesus took his human place in the rich tradition of tradesmen in the Hebrew nation.

The Jewish people had many skilled tradesmen; they made treasured well-made articles. These trades, including that of carpenter, also developed into arts. When directions were given for the building of the temple, "cunning work" was encouraged, including "the cutting of stones" and "carving in wood." The woodcarving included the pillars and curved capitals of the temple, the paneling of cedar, the roof of pine, the doors of olive wood, the designs in sandalwood and boxwood. Since many of these woods were quite rare in Palestine, the work of the carpenter was highly skilled and prized. Moreover, by the presence of such ornate designs in the temple, we can see that the arts are one means by which we can glorify God.

By the time of Jesus, who followed in the trade of his father Joseph, carpentry had come to include many tasks. A skilled carpenter undertook all the tasks of building, framing doors and windows, and fitting roofs. Finely wrought furniture and kitchen utensils of the time still survive today. Seeing samples of that furniture today, one marvels at the tools used to produce them. These included a marking tool called a "rule," the adz for chiseling, saws, files, and hammers. A primitive copper bit was turned as a drill by a bow and leather thong to make the dowel joints of furniture.

We see, then, that our Savior did significant, demanding work. He could not have done such work in a slap-dash fashion. Many of us have tried a do-it-yourself project that looked all too much like something we did ourselves.

I am far from being an expert carpenter, but I have always loved trying. Some of my tools are old, nearly antiques, handed down through several generations. When I first cut into a two by four, I pause and savor the sweet richness of its odor. I slow down, finding my way as I go. In this slow, methodical way, however, I have tackled (and finished!) some large projects, including building two family rooms (I'm starting to get the hang of them), a bedroom addition, and two complete kitchen remodelings. One thing I've learned is that a carpenter can't be in a hurry. Mistakes pop up like leprechauns, waving their hats and making funny faces.

In fact, I've learned that you have to give in to the task in a way—let the materials have *their* way with you. Learn to work with them.

I am reminded of Isaiah's confession, "We are the clay, you are the potter" (64:8). We might paraphrase this, "Lord, we are the wood, you are our carpenter." Especially during this Lenten season, we want to be molded and conformed to Jesus' will.

Jesus the carpenter was human among humans, laboring, sweating over the carpenter's bench, crafting the piece for beauty and strength. In so doing, Jesus also dignifies all our work, which we are called to do carefully and well. That is the remarkable wonder of Jesus the carpenter: that God came among us and lived as we do. But far richer is this fact: that day by day Jesus molds us to his will as we submit to his tender hands.

Hebrews 11:10

For [Abraham] was looking forward to the city with foundations, whose artitect and builder is God.

Prayer

Abraham had the great faith.
He looked forward to the city built by God,
but his life work was building that city among humans.
I am no Abraham,
but I join him in that work;
quietly—not always confidently,
deliberately—not always successfully.
I pray you, Jesus, to take my faulty effort
and translate it by your skill
into a temple fit for your dwelling.
Amen.

THE CARPENTER:
THE DIVINE BUILDER

We picture the carpenter against the frame of a new house or crafting a fine piece of furniture. Some of us may think of volunteer service with Habitat for Humanity or a similar federation. One might picture the carpenter in an altogether different way, however.

I grew up in an area of Michigan that forms a spawning ground for tornadoes. The confluence of air currents from the cold reaches of the Arctic and from the hot, wet reaches of the Gulf of Mexico tends, at certain seasons, to collide over Lake Michigan. The forces crash together to breed tornadoes with too great a frequency. When children return to school in the fall, one of the first lessons is "What to do in a tornado drill"—a lesson repeated in the spring. They practice diving under desks with arms over their heads, or running into the hallways.

Having lived through a "big one" still haunts my memory. It came during the first year Pat and I were married, also my last at college. I had been working in the college library on a May afternoon when the desk before me appeared strangely dim. I glanced at my watch, thinking I had worked through supper, and began to pack up my books. Suddenly someone shouted. The ghostly hush was broken by the terrifying words, "Tornado sky!"

We moved—and moved fast. The sirens were blasting as I raced my old car home.

That was a foolish move. Everyone knows that you run to a basement or hallway, put your arms over you head. But newlyweds are not normal people. I wanted to get home to Pat.

A green-throated monster stalked the whole western sky, eating up incredible space. Save for the pounding of my car engine and the wail of sirens, the world was silent. Black tongues flickered out of a blacker heart, thrusting down. The air was thick. It was hard to breathe. I pulled the car to a slewing stop before the apartment and ran up the steps, calling to Pat. She was just jumping out of the bathtub and, taking only enough time to throw on a bathrobe, raced with me to the cellar. We no sooner jumped down the steps than the first tornado hit, a sound like locomotives blown apart by the fury of their own pent-up power. Strange, shrill noises rose above it. The crash of trees, the sound of things ripping apart, echoed while those wind-claws touched down and gouged the earth.

Save for a foot of water that rose in the basement under the torrential rains, we escaped untouched. But the next morning revealed a chaos of debris. For blocks about us, houses stood with roofs pried off like soup cans, huge trees lay uprooted, and brush and grass littered the streets. Shards of wood were driven at terrific force like bullets and stood imbedded in sides of houses. The freakish, unpredictable power of the storm moved cars, upended some, left others untouched.

After such a storm, crews of carpenters worked day and night to restore order. Out of such desolate frightening loss, they brought about a certain peace. They would put things right.

Somewhat in this same spirit of restoring things to order after desolating loss, Amos prophesies the coming of the carpenter, the builder. The profession of Jesus as carpenter, we begin to understand, was not just an earthly occupation but also a divine calling. Amos (9:11–12) writes:

"In that day I will restore
    David's fallen tent.
I will repair its broken places,
    restore its ruins,
    and build it up as it used to be,
so that they may possess the remnant of Edom
    and all the nations that bear my name,"
        declares the LORD, who will do these things.

The prophecy of the builder appears elsewhere in the Old Testament. For example, David writes in Psalm 102:16, "For the LORD will rebuild Zion / and appear in his glory." In reference to these prophecies, Jesus announces his task as the builder in John 2:19, "Jesus answered them, 'Destroy this temple, and I will raise it again in three days.'"

Just how does that affect us, however? We know now that Jesus is the master builder, and that he will prepare or build a place for us. Yet, just like those carpenters who showed up after the tornado to rebuild the neighborhood, a far deeper and more profound solace appears in this name of Jesus. Consider that one of the more skilled and delicate tasks of the carpenter was also the art of engraving. Suddenly that verse in Isaiah 49:16 makes sense, "I have engraved you on the palms of my hands." There we rest secure. We cannot be eradicated from his fierce grip of grace. But have we ever understood *how* we are graven in the palms of God's hands? It was through the divine work of Jesus the carpenter.

Consider this. They took the carpenter and placed him against the wood he loved. Then the soldiers picked up the carpenter's tools, the hammer and the nails. They did not handle the worn tools carefully and lovingly. This was a work to be done quickly. They grasped the tools roughly, like novices, anxious to get on with the job. The nail was a jagged spike, meant to be driven harshly to hold a joint tight. The spike was driven into Jesus' palms, where the hand meets the wrist, nailing the carpenter to the wood. His own tools turned on him. And thereby we, in the blows of the hammer on the spike, are *graven* on the palms of God's hands. Each blow of the hammer strikes our own name there: "For your sins he died."

Jesus, the carpenter. It is more than just a name; more than just a trade. Across the gulf of time and eternity, Jesus the carpenter fashioned a bridge in the shape of the cross. Allowing himself to be nailed to it—so that he *became* the cross, so that the carpenter became the divinely crafted work—Jesus gave us a way to be carried safely across that gulf, in his palms upon which our names are graven by the carpenter's nails.

Psalm 107:28–30

Then they cried out to the LORD in their trouble,
    and he brought them out of their distress.
He stilled the storm to a whisper;
    the waves of the sea were hushed.
They were glad when it grew calm,
    and he guided them to their desired haven.

Prayer

I confess I am afraid when the storms
wrack my life. I name them to you, O God,
I give them all over to your keeping,
and you hear my cry above the beating waves.
I thank you for making a way in the sea.
I thank you for making the storms be still.
And even when the sea-billows do roll,
I thank you, Jesus, for making it well with my soul.
I thank you that all this is possible
Only because you have my name
Engraved in the powerful grip of your hand.
Amen.

Day Five

BUILDER OF THE WORLD

orced to honesty, at some time or other we have all probably felt as if a tornado has blasted through our lives, leaving us on shaky ground. Perhaps I should speak for myself, for those moments when I have felt bereft of God's presence. At times I seem to hear only the howling of the wind and realize that it is only my own mind thudding against its spherical walls. At such times, I pump some familiar truths into my mind like CPR.

I listen to Isaiah say, "Was it not you who dried up the sea, / the waters of the great deep, / who made a road in the depths of the sea / so that the redeemed might cross over?" (51:10). I think, that is good, Isaiah. But why, just five verses later, does he add, " For I am the LORD… / who churns up the sea so that its waves roar" (51:15). Now, that doesn't seem quite fair. Why can't we just have a gentle sea, with average waves?

Then too, there is that great promise God delivers through Isaiah, "I have engraved you on the palms of my hands" (49:16). Security and comfort lie in the mighty hand of God. Why, then, do I sometimes feel like Job, that the hand has turned into a fist upon me. The great Jesuit poet Gerard Manley Hopkins asked in "Carrion Comfort," "Why wouldst thou [be] rude on me?" Indeed, why? Like Hopkins, I have felt the "lion limb" strike me.

Unexpected twists and turns rip at the sinews of our spiritual belief. Where do I go when sense scrambles and Humpty Dumpty has a smirk on his lopsided face? I go to meet God, in a place where time slows, and God's spirit speaks. For me it is a garden.

At the big old house on Neland Avenue where I grew up, the lawn was pretty much nature's lost cause. The grass was cut maybe twice a year—haphazardly at that. My father struggled powerfully, like Adam after the Fall, to make something presentable of the front yard. Once he trucked in a load of black dirt. He applied enough bags of organic fertilizer that the yard stunk half the summer. A few valiant stems of grass actually rustled among the weeds for all his effort.

But along the south side of the house, between the house and the driveway, he grew his gardens, and they were magnificent. From a colleague who lived on a farm, my father hauled baskets of manure in the trunk of the old Ford. He dug deep, mixing in good dirt. Nothing but the best. From May to October that garden blazed with beauty. I remember him getting up from the study desk by the windows that overlooked the garden, at any time his heart prompted him, and wandering out to that magical space to work in the soil.

My mother never touched a flower, not even to cut them. Nonetheless, my parents' four offspring all inherited the love for soil and living things.

It is almost like redemption—this gardening. It frees you from, and it frees you for. If someone should ask me what I am doing in the garden at any given moment during the day, in honesty I would have to say, "thinking." I am away from the desk—freed, perhaps, from some problem that arose in writing. When the fingers get busy with some plant or weed instead of the cold, metallic feel of the pen or keyboard, a different kind of thinking comes. I'm freed *for,* as dark earth creeps under the fingernails, and the juice of weeds stains my fingers. When I return to the desk, there are often so many words sprung out of the scent of roses that the pen has a hard time keeping up.

I am freed *for* quiet. I am freed by the slow, mechanical nature of my tasks to empty my thoughts, set aside anxiety and stress, and let God's voice fill those troubled spots.

That is how I work the garden, steadily and slowly. Mostly the soil is smooth and dark and flaky with years of compost turned into it. Nonetheless, it is a drawing place that is as close as the porch door. When I am there, knees in the damp grass, I wonder if God ever worked the gardens of his new world into shape this way, thumbing out a maze of hills and valleys like silly putty, palming a glacier to smooth out great plains for the buffalo to roam, separating the firmament in just such a way that it left thousands of lakes for loons and fat bears and walleye to play in. I know God created at a word, but don't tell me he didn't have a world of fun doing it.

The Master Builder is also none other than the Master Gardener of our world.

Psalm 33:20–22

We wait in hope for the LORD;
    he is our help and our shield.
In him our hearts rejoice,
    for we trust in his holy name.
May your unfailing love rest upon us, O LORD,
    even as we put our hope in you.

Prayer

What matchless love is this, dear Jesus,
ever faithful, ever true?
In this world of change
and the furious swirl.
I pray that I will be
ever faithful to you.
May I hold my eyes upon you,
and will you keep me,
as the work you have made me,
always under your loving gaze.
Amen.

Day Six

THE CARPENTER:
A WORK FOR THE WORLD

I sn't it reasonable to say that Jesus' profession as carpenter brought him into a uniquely personal relationship with those dying of sin in this world? The carpenter, after all, both repairs the bent and warped places but also builds anew. Like a nurse caring for a patient, the carpenter, finally, makes for other people.

Any true craftsman takes pride and pleasure in his or her own work, just as we do in our own if we are truly called to it. The work itself comes to represent that carpenter, to the degree that some fine pieces of furniture, much like a painting or other work of art, bears the name of the master craftsman. So, too, some people point with pride to the fact that a certain builder constructed their house. Curiously enough, however, the carpenter's work is always for others. Someone else will "own" that piece of furniture; someone else will live in that house. Nonetheless, it bears the mark of the one who made it, and is identified as his or hers.

While I was in graduate school, married, and with two children during the last year, I paid the bills that my scholarship didn't cover in a time-honored way among teachers—summertime painting of houses. I fancied myself a good painter, and apparently others thought so, too. I never had to advertise and always had more than enough work to cover those bills that had accumulated.

Still, there were jobs I wish I had turned down. Like the three-story house with the ornate little dormers on the roof. I had to climb to the top rungs of my ladder and, cautiously but precariously, clamber over them to the angled roof. Or like that house built along the edge of a cliff with a hundred-foot drop-off, so that the ladder, staked down with ropes and cinches, perched on the very edge of the bluff. It didn't help that the house was in a town called Slippery Rock.

The work was always hot, often messy, and certainly quite fearful atop those swaying ladders. But I loved it—so much so that I continued with a few other young teachers during my first few years of teaching. Painting a house changes its personality. It is a creative work, the making of a new thing. Maybe even my own overcoming of the frustration I felt in third grade when the teacher handed up lumps of clay and said, "Now make something." I made a horse and she mistook it for a football. With house painting I could make this new thing.

As I gained confidence and pleasure in my house painting, I figured this work of art I was crafting deserved the artist's signature. I began signing my houses before completing the job. Not on a lower wall, of course. Under the eave forty feet off the ground, or on the edge of a storm window before it was placed in the frame. Places only I knew about—until the next painter would see it and stand perplexed at this odd thing.

The carpenter, the expert craftsman, invariably leaves an individual mark upon the work, but the work finally is for others. As a carpenter Jesus surely must have experienced this. After laboring with the adz and saw, the chisels and hammers, did he hold the work up to the light, eyeing each line for conformity, testing each joint for strength? Did the shavings from the shop cling to his clothes and on his hands and wrists? And did he hand the work with pride and satisfaction to the purchaser? One dares imagine no less.

In a far deeper sense, however, Jesus the carpenter performed his masterwork on Calvary. This work was one of eternal design that he purchased himself, that he gave freely as a gift to whomever reaches to take it. Those houses I painted will have to be repainted one day, and the painter will receive his check for the labor. But this masterwork of Jesus never diminishes and is always at the same price, costing not less than everything, a price he already paid.

Jesus the Carpenter fashioned this new work, this eternal building, stretched across the span of wood on the crest of Golgotha. He was not providing just a remodeling project, however. As sinners, we are not good enough simply to be "redecorated," to have a few loose or warped ends straightened. Romans 3:23–24 tells us that "all have sinned and fall short of the glory of God, and are justified freely by his grace through the redemption that came by Christ Jesus." This miraculous reconstruction project calls for a whole new person. So it is that Paul writes, "[I]f anyone is in Christ, he is a new creation" (2 Corinthians 5:17). The rebuilding by Jesus the Carpenter makes us wholly new, strips us down, and constructs a whole new foundation for living.

As a new construction, his mark is also upon us. We bear the signature of Jesus: "I have [called] you by name," says the Lord in Isaiah 43:1, "you are mine." Remade by the Christ, we bear his name —Christians.

John 15:12–14

"My command is this: Love each other as I have loved you. Greater love has no one than this, that he lay down his life for his friends. You are my friends if you do what I command."

Prayer

Forgive me, Lord Jesus, for those times
when I have turned, full of your priceless gift,
to the world and offered nothing.
Forgive me for the closed hand and closed heart.
Teach me, Lord, to give as you have given,
to be friends with the friendless,
to love those who are unloved or unloving.
Amen.

THE PRECIOUS STONE

Since childhood years I have loved to travel to northern Michigan. To recall that time, I once took my own family camping far into the northern peninsula until we ended at the last branch of land into Lake Superior—as far north as we could go.

More often, however, we take a short camping or motel trip up to one of the small towns or campgrounds along the Lake Michigan shore. Each holds its individual charm. If you visit Traverse City, for example, you can turn northwest and follow the bay through rolling groves of cherry trees, their spring petals like colorful clouds caught in black branches. We drive through the old fishing village of Northport and along roads you wouldn't know unless someone had given you directions. Fortunately we have directions. Longtime friends have a summer cottage in the area, and they also long ago gave us a key to it.

The shoreline along the Traverse Bay has no sandy beaches; one must drive to the Lake Michigan side for that. Nonetheless, it is one of the most fascinating shorelines I have ever walked. It is really a large treasure box that invites you in for a treasure hunt.

Here is the way we hunt. We wear old sneakers, for one thing. We're walking on stones, some broken and jagged. Sometimes the old tennis shoes come out lacerated. We walk in water about six inches deep. That way we can pick out the treasures that the waves wash over on the shore side and also those in slightly deeper water.

We are looking for Petoskey stones. When they lie underwater, these prehistoric fossils glitter with intricate patterns, as beguiling as an intricate puzzle. When dry, they seem like any common, grayish stone. One wouldn't give them a second glance.

Others who know where and how to look may take them home and polish them to a lustrous glow with rock polishers or the hand method of fine sandpaper and jeweler's rouge. We have bags of unpolished stones in the garage. Some of the nicer ones I dump in the fish tank; a few I've polished the easy way—a coat of polyurethane—and keep them on the windowsill in my office. Always, they are reminders. Not only of our travels but also of the beauty that can lie under a dusty skin. Although they may be largely reminders to me, I have often seen people in my office almost automatically reach out to one of the stones, admire its beauty, peer closely at its multiple variegations of fossil imprints, and turn its smooth surface over with searching fingers. Inevitably if they are not Michigan natives, they wonder about the stone's origin.

For such people the Petoskey stone holds certain lessons. First, one must know what they are, that the fossil imprints occurred at some point beyond our counting when God caused the great glaciers to shift and scour the soil. (I like to think of it as part of the separation of the dry land from the water.) Then, one has to know where to find them. One has to go toward them to receive their gift, to discover their beauty under the dusty skin. Then, too, one must know their intrinsic worth. Truly, tourist shops by the dozens in Michigan coastal towns sell the highly polished stones. They arrive from the polishing drums looking like buffed jewels. But a Petoskey stone is not simply a bauble to behold, like a piece of costume jewelry. It holds an inner, only partially revealed, beauty. One really comes to treasure it by, say, dipping a wet finger on it, watching the patterns mysteriously come to life with a profound beauty.

And finally, one should be aware of its enduring beauty. Like diamonds locked as carbon deposits deep in the earth, Petoskey stones wash mysteriously from the depths and storms of Lake Michigan. When you hold one, you get the feeling that something incredibly old, beyond time's reckoning, is present here and now. It is very nearly a feeling of awe.

Interestingly, God who made these Petoskey stones often reveals himself or his special relationship with humanity through stones.

For example, when God called Moses to the mountaintop to reveal his commandments for human living, the message was inscribed on tablets of stone. The enduring and beautiful promises of God are inscribed on stone to signify that they are not momentary and passing, but enduring as rock.

Similarly, God revealed his faithful mercy when he ordered Moses to strike the rock at Horeb and sweet water flowed out of it. Here the stone provided physical nourishment, and, in the searing desert, life itself.

As one turns to the more prophetic books of the Old Testament, however, the references to stones take on a more expectant, urgent, and searching tone. It is almost as if we are wading the lakeshore, looking for that one Petoskey stone couched among so many common rocks. Some of the same lessons, in fact, also seem to apply as we search out the cornerstone of our faith. In this case, it is the living presence of Jesus himself.

Jesus is the living stone, into whom we are mortared for our spiritual life. We find him not among the shops and splendors of this life, but revealed in God's word and in our very lives. We find Jesus in a relationship. As such, this precious cornerstone bears intrinsic worth; that is, he alone is the source of our spiritual relationship. As God released the sweet water from the rock at Horeb, so he releases the living water to us through Jesus. No striking of the rock occurred; instead, the whips stripped the flesh that, as Isaiah wrote, bore our grief and carried our sorrows (see 53:4). Above all, this rock Jesus bears enduring beauty. Surely he was bruised and disfigured in *this* life like a dusty gray Petoskey stone lying on the dry shore. Few imagined the beauty he carried. But then we realize that Jesus is not, indeed, some prehistoric fossil, but a living presence at this moment, at this place. He is not time-bound in any sense. Jesus is eternal God, who saw fit to enter our time briefly to do his mighty work of eternal salvation.

Here is the mystery, and the consummate beauty, of the One who is our cornerstone.

I lift the Petoskey stone off the shelf, feeling its smooth contours under my fingers. I dip its surface with moisture and watch the mysterious whorls appear. It almost seems that the stone reaches back with its inner life. Beauty beyond the superficial; beauty beyond comprehension.

In the same mysterious way I reach out to God, and find Jesus reaching back to me, my name engraved on the palms of his hands.

1 Peter 2:4–5

As you come to him, the living Stone—rejected by men but chosen by God and precious to him—you also, like living stones, are being built into a spiritual house to be a holy priesthood, offering spiritual sacrifices acceptable to God through Jesus Christ.

Prayer

My Jesus, I love thee,
I know thou art mine.
That song is in my heart today,
Lord—with thanksgiving
for the bruised beauty you carried to the cross
which made me redeemed,
precious, and of infinite worth
in your sight.
Amen.

Day Eight

THE SECURITY OF STONE

A wrenching paradox infiltrates every moment of the Lenten season. We liken the preciousness of a stone to the preciousness of Jesus and his love for us. Yet he was battered and bruised and killed to obtain that preciousness. Jesus intervened with those superpious scribes and Pharisees from stoning a woman caught in the act of adultery. As the leaders quarreled around him, Jesus simply traced words in the dust, then said, "If any one of you is without sin, let him be the first to throw a stone at her" (John 8:7). Within moments, these same legalists turned their rage of propriety on Jesus himself. They press Jesus about who his father is, and, finally, Jesus names himself by the very name that God gave to Moses at the burning bush—"I tell you the truth…before Abraham was born, I am!" (John 8:58). The keepers of the Law now grab stones to rain them down on the Lord of heaven and earth. What a paradox! How does one stone God?

Only if God willingly gives himself up to it.

The paradoxes of Lenten stones don't end there, however. All those long years before Jesus was ever born, Isaiah, also paraphrasing King David, made this prophecy:

> …this is what the Sovereign LORD says:
> See, I lay a stone in Zion,
>   a tested stone,
> a precious cornerstone for a sure foundation;
>   the one who trusts will never be dismayed (28:16).

To understand the unfolding paradoxes of this prophecy in the New Testament, and how they reveal something of our Savior to us, it is necessary to probe into the nature of that precious cornerstone.

The cornerstone is so named because it serves as the foundational link in two intersecting walls. One could accurately say it is the most important stone in the structure because, first, it unifies, and second, it supports. If the stone isn't absolutely true, the walls in the building will weaken, fall out of alignment, and eventually collapse. The cornerstone itself, then, must consist of a hard, enduring stone that will not be subject to the wear of weather or time.

The problem was that stones work two ways, and here also lies the paradox. While the cornerstone unified and supported the stones or bricks mortared to it, those who don't see the cornerstone for what it is can stumble over it. While the mason selects the cornerstone as a precious piece, others might ignore it or despise it as something in the way.

Make no mistake: Jesus is in the way. You can't get around him, or over him, or sneak past him. Yet, this is precisely what so many humans try to do. They play with their fuzzy, mystical gods, or they pretend there is no God at all. Some even play a game with Christianity, treating it like a trading card they can turn in for admission at some heavenly portal. Every soul ever created has to go directly before him and there recognize that he is either the stumbling stone, as Romans 9:32 has it, or the precious cornerstone. There won't be any question at that moment.

Does that worry us? It need not, for there is more about this cornerstone. In this case, it is a gravestone.

When they hung Jesus, that scourged and bloody wreck of a human being, surely those in power thought they had finally gotten rid of the troublemaker. The Pharisees, who had sought his death for months, could now go back to their temples and relax. The Roman soldiers—well, they had done their job. The disciples were scattered. It is, as he himself said, finished.

But if Satan had bruised Jesus' heel, Jesus had crushed Satan's head.

Here's the rest of the story of the Precious Stone.

When Jesus' body was ripped from the cross—the rough wood structure upended and fallen to the ground, the nails pried out from inert flesh—a wealthy man named Joseph came forward. Since he had become a disciple of Jesus, he wanted to bury his Lord in a tomb on his own land. The tomb was cut out of rock, never before used. In fact, Joseph had intended it for himself, but he gave himself up for his Lord—just as his Lord had given himself up for Joseph. Carefully Joseph wrapped the body in clean linen, placed it in the tomb, and then, as was the custom to keep predators away, rolled a large stone over the entrance to secure the tomb. If that wasn't enough, the chief priests and Pharisees, remembering Jesus' claim that he would rise in three days, sealed the tomb in place and posted a guard at it.

The paradox is nearly laughable. The cornerstone of all creation sealed by a stone mortared in place. A few drowsy guards keeping watch. The tomb wasn't then, nor is it ever, the end of the story. For the second time in three days the earth shook violently—once at Jesus' death, again at his resurrection. An angel so brilliant in appearance that he seemed like a bolt of lightning rolled that stone away and sat on it. It is as if the Lord of heaven now said, "I have conquered death once and for all! Here I am."

Scripture tells us that the first reaction of those disciples to the risen Christ was often fear. Over and over Jesus or his angels say, "Don't be afraid." His message to us during this Lenten season is precisely the same. In his "high priestly prayer" recorded in John 14:17, Jesus foresees his crucifixion and uses the moment to speak words of peace into the hearts of his troubled disciples. The theme of that entire prayer may well be summarized by John 14:27, "Peace I leave with you; my peace I give to you. I do not give as the world gives. Do not let your hearts be troubled and do not be afraid."

There arise moments in our lives when our place on the precious cornerstone seems insecure, when troubles and fear assault us from every direction, and the walls are collapsing all around us. That is the time when these words spoken by the Rock of our Salvation (see Psalm 62:2) are held precious in our ears.

1 John 4:18–19

There is no fear in love. But perfect love drives out fear, because fear has to do with punishment. The one who fears is not made perfect in love.

We love because he first loved us.

Prayer

How can I say thanks
for all the love you have shown to me?
There are no choirs on all earth,
no songs of praise sufficient,
not enough words in my vocabulary—
but only this: I love you, Lord,
for you have first loved me,
and driven out my fear.
Amen.

Day Nine

REMEMBER THE STONE

There is one more chapter in the story about stones.

It begins with Joshua after the death of Moses. Joshua had inherited a stubborn and stiff-necked people, as Moses frequently called them. Assuming leadership over these people buckled Joshua's courage. I imagine he thought something like, "Who am I to lead these people?" And perhaps he also thought, "I don't want anything to do with leading this people."

No doubt many of us can identify with such thoughts. We sometimes get drawn into messy situations where the weight of decision and authority rests too heavily on our shoulders. We would rather pass on it, delegate it to someone else. Who am I to lead these people?

God is fully aware of Joshua's reluctance. He speaks powerful words into Joshua's heart: "As I was with Moses, so I will be with you; I will never leave you nor forsake you" (1:5). Based on *that* promise of his presence, God tells Joshua, not once but four times, "Be strong and courageous" (verses 6, 7, 9, 18). The encouragement is decidedly at odds with the modern mind, which so often searches for the quickest and easiest way out. During my two years of military service, I heard one slogan over and over: Never volunteer for anything. Stay cool; slide into the background; get by in the easiest way possible.

I suspect that Joshua would have liked to have done just that. But he has a promise from God, and he has encouragement from God. He picks up the leadership of Moses and leads the people into the promised land. To do so, however, he has to cross the Jordan River. That's when the challenges start. The Jordan is at flood stage. There aren't any boats around to ferry the hundreds of thousands of Israelites. What now, Lord? "Be strong and courageous."

God provides the direction. The priests, carrying the Ark of the Covenant signifying God's presence, take a half-mile head start on the people. As soon as they set foot into the Jordan, the upstream waters backed up in a wall. You have to go into the water before anything happens. "Be strong and courageous."

What "happened" was that the whole nation of Israel crossed on dry, firm ground. While the priests still stood—firm and dry—Joshua appointed twelve men, one from each of the tribes, to go *back* into the middle of the Jordan and lift a stone out of its bed. These weren't mere pebbles. They were stones the men hefted to their shoulders and carried back to the shore. Why bother?

They laid the stones alongside the Jordan as a memorial altar. Joshua makes it clear: "In the future, when your children ask you, 'What do these stones mean?' tell them that the flow of the Jordan was cut off before the ark of the covenant of the LORD" (4:6–7). The stones, he adds, "are to be a memorial to the people of Israel forever." Forever? I suspect that no matter how hard one tried, using all of our modern technology, one could not find that altar of twelve stones alongside the Jordan. So when our children ask, "What do these stones mean?" how do we answer?

In the twenty-first chapter of Revelation, the New Jerusalem is unveiled for our seeing. This is the city built on the cornerstone of Jesus. It is the city purchased for us by his blood. It is a city with no more weeping, with no more dying, and with dazzling beauty. At the heart of that beauty lie the twelve precious stones. They symbolize God's amazing grace to Joshua's Israelites just as the cornerstone represents Jesus' amazing grace to each one of us.

What, then, do these stones mean?

That our acts of faith, those times we step out in courage, are a glory to the heavenly city of Christ the King, for one thing. What might seem to us merely a routine deed—lifting the stone of someone else's burden—when placed on the altar of our love for Jesus now becomes precious.

Revelation 21:22–23

I did not see a temple in the city, because the Lord God Almighty and the Lamb are its temple. The city does not need the sun or the moon to shine on it, for the glory of God gives it light, and the Lamb is its lamp.

Prayer

When I feel weak,
my energy like a gray March fog,
my soul like puddles in the parking lot,
let me hear your voice saying,
"Be brave and have courage—
I am your God."
I rest my life on the altar
of your grace, Lord.
Amen.

THE COMFORTER

When God said, "Comfort, comfort my people," those words came in a stormy time for his people. The great Assyrian empire marched on the Israelite nation, devouring huge chunks of it with ease. As the Israelite people shrank as a nation, their faith also shriveled. Who can help against such a foe as the Assyrians? Moreover, with the exception of the godly king Hezekiah, the highest positions in government were rat's nests of iniquity. Moral integrity collapsed from the top down.

In this madness, Isaiah dares to speak of comfort?

In the case of the Israelites, that comfort did not mean that the situation immediately changed. In fact, it only grew worse as the Persian kingdom entered the fray and began hauling the Israelites off into exile like so many cattle. Things couldn't get much lower for "God's chosen people" when they now became the chosen laughingstock of the nations.

> Comfort, comfort my people,
> > says your God.
> Speak tenderly to Jerusalem,
> > and proclaim to her
> that her hard service has been completed,
> > that her sin has been paid for,
> that she has received from the LORD's hand
> > double for all her sins (Isaiah 40:1–2).

The situation doesn't immediately change for the Israelites, but the comfort suggests that something in their hearts does.

Here is also where our own confusion can grow. We want comfort *by having the situation changed.* That is our human yearning, and it seems unfathomable that any comfort can quiet our hearts unless the situation changes.

If the Old Testament promise of comfort confuses us between our desire for a change in situation and the promise of comfort for a change of heart, it seems at first glance that Jesus' words on comfort confuse the issue further. As he so often did, Jesus tripped all our human understanding upside down. He pointed out, in fact, that when our situation seems to be going absolutely splendidly, when we are in our own eyes exquisitely comfortable, our hearts are in gravest danger. In his series of "blessings and curses" recorded in Luke 6, Jesus lists his series of woes: "But woe to you who are rich, / for you have already received your comfort. / Woe to you who are well fed now, / for you will go hungry" (24–25). Throughout the successive woes, the point is the same. Worldly comfort is not the same as—and in fact often destroys—spiritual comfort.

What comfort may we draw from our Comforter during the season when we lay ourselves spiritually naked before the cross? We strip away the social poses now. We don't dare come as anything other than what we truly are.

To understand this, return to Isaiah for a moment as he prophesied comfort in the stormiest of times, when moral authority disintegrates and individual hearts spin with loneliness and confusion. Precisely at that moment, Isaiah testifies most mightily to God's presence. In chapter 43, Isaiah proclaims our one and only Savior, our only sure comfort, in words that still ring down through the ages in authenticity and power:

"Fear not, for I have redeemed you;
  I have summoned you by name; you are mine.
When you pass through the waters,
  I will be with you;
and when you pass through the rivers,
  they will not sweep over you.
When you walk through the fire,
  you will not be burned;
  the flames will not set you ablaze.
For I am the LORD, your God,
  the Holy One of Israel, your Savior"
(Isaiah 43:1–3).

The passage does not say that we will be miraculously extricated from those situations that confuse us. The rivers of tribulation will continue to roll, and the fires of trials will continue to blaze in our lifetimes. But God is there, by our side, walking with us.

When Jesus walked to Golgotha and the cross, he walked alone. No one could do this work with or for him. He was utterly forsaken. The cross now is his invitation to walk alongside him. In his prayer for believers, Jesus promises that "I will not leave you as orphans; I will come to you" (John 14:18). And, echoing Isaiah, he gives this benediction, "Peace I leave with you; my peace I give to you. I do not give as the world gives. Do not let your hearts be troubled and do not be afraid" (14:27).

There rests our comfort. No matter what our situation, the Lord of Life walks with us through it, speaking peace into our troubled hearts.

2 Corinthians 1:6

If we are distressed, it is for your comfort and salvation; if we are comforted, it is for your comfort, which produces in you patient endurance of the same sufferings we suffer.

Prayer

My life is in your hands—
secure and safe.
You are my comforter
when all around me things fail,
slip into tumult,
roll wildly like rivers at flood stage.
Thank you for the peace
of the cross that surpasses
all my understanding.
Amen.

THE COMFORTER:
IN LONELINESS

I t is one thing to talk about the comfort of God as some abstract concept, or even as a theological and doctrinal truth. Who, after all, wants to believe in a God who fails to comfort or has little concern for his own creation? Christianity is a love-driven religion, based on a relationship between believers and their God. This is the special awareness of every moment of Lent.

Even though we might perfectly understand that comfort in a theological, doctrinal way, it takes on personal significance in our relationship when it meets us at the point of our deepest need. Therefore, it is also fitting during these Lenten meditations to probe our need and God's response to it.

Chief among those deeply human hurts that shape our need, I believe, is loneliness. Perhaps I am particularly aware of this as a college teacher where I find many young people wandering a maze of uncertainty and loneliness. It reminds me of the paradox of the forest, for I am deeply drawn to them, willing to hike far into them, but also aware of the risks of getting lost.

Some people have an internal compass that is calibrated and magnetized as perfectly as a precision instrument. Like Augustine's idealized state of humanity where it will not be possible to sin—*non posse peccare*—for these people it is not possible to get lost. But Augustine, that one-time hard and eager sinner, also knew that he appreciated the expectation of his idealized state simply because for him it was, at one time, not possible not to sin—*non posse non peccare*. Perhaps those people with perfect internal guidance have missed something.

When I look for moss on the north sides of a tree trunk, I find only trees with moss all around. I've discovered this is nearly always the case in the deep forest, where the shadows are so thick moss grows where it will. When I look for stars to guide my way, I get lost in their light and forget the guidance. When I need the sun to guide me, it is either directly overhead or obscured by cloud. Yet, I have been lost in the forest only once.

I didn't panic. In fact, I rather enjoyed it, walking along, calling out once in a while. It got tiring in time, but not panicky. After all, I knew this forest was only a few miles in any direction. After a time others found me. The signs were so clear when they pointed them out: Don't you remember that fallen tree? That bluff with the brush that looks like a stocking hat? That rock that points like an arrow the way you should have gone? And I did after they were pointed out. But what I remember now is the joy of rejoining those I love.

In the northern forests one is often, as Henri Nouwen calls it in his memorable *Genesee Diary*, "alone with the Alone." It took the forests of New York to teach him that. But we are also often alone with others, and sometimes solitude makes loving others easier. For a time, we are no longer judged by the world's standards, and it is easier to reach out and hold someone's hand, to hug someone, to say, "I love you."

But then I found the lesson I had really been looking for among the big trees.

We are never really lost, nor really alone. When God said to Joshua, "I will never leave you nor forsake you" (1:5), God wasn't making idle chatter. He made a promise. He is the one with us, making that same promise today.

2 Corinthians 1:3–4

Praise be to the God and Father of our Lord Jesus Christ, the Father of compassion and the God of all comfort, who comforts us in all our troubles, so that we can comfort those in any trouble with the comfort we…[receive] from God.

Prayer

Lord, I pray for myself
but especially for others—
for those who are lonely
for those who feel friendless and forsaken—
and that I may have the grace
to reach out with a word or a hand
in Jesus' name to bring them comfort
on this day.
Amen.

Day Twelve

THE COMFORTER:
IN AGING

When I learned as a child to honor my parents, I never had much trouble doing that. They were, after all, honorable parents. Even though the normal quarrels and "difference of opinions" occurred in our family, it was a home where Christ held prominence and love was evident.

That family life was marked by rituals and routines that made it special—from my father's early awakening each morning and singing in the kitchen while he brewed coffee (a singing that he thought was private but that worked its way up the hollow walls of that old house until each of us was awake) to my mother's near-constant baking in that same small kitchen. Some people believe rituals deaden life. To some extent, this may be true. When our worship, for example, becomes *merely* ritual, it is a sign of spiritual need.

But rituals also ground our lives in meaningful patterns. They grant familiarity and ties of love. We can all identify with these. In our family, for example, it has always been a ritual to gather for Sunday dinner. By doing so, we retain cords to a mysterious past and tie them to a present mystery of love.

Before my father passed away (a decade after my mother), he arrived for Sunday dinner precisely at 12:30. I waited by the side door for the sound of his coming. When the car stopped, I opened the door to the porch and stepped out to greet him.

I waited because my father was aging, strong shoulders hunched and thin, his gait unsteady, and because there are three steps up into the house. He climbed them by himself at a sort of shaking trot. I would not dream of helping him. I am strong enough to catch my father as he climbed up ahead of me. Only three steps.

I waited by the side door, the sound of the car coming down the street. He will be gripping the steering wheel with hands frozen tight together at the top of the wheel, accelerator and brake pressed down simultaneously as the car ground to a stop.

I remember him as a young driver, as a young father, who drove the beaten hulks that were our cars to the point of collapse. He kept his foot off the brake then, so the accelerator was free to do what he wanted.

I had a boyhood dentist who, since he was also my uncle, gave the family cut-rate fees. In a tiny second-story office above a saloon (we entered by the back door of the saloon up a flight of stairs), he wrought havoc upon the mouths of kin and strangers alike. For five dollars a filling he jacked holes all over my teeth, most of which fell out and had to be restored for exorbitant sums within ten years. By then he had died. He didn't have a refund policy anyway.

While this criminal activity (felonious assault) went on above the saloon, my father, after dropping me off, went looking for the nearest bookstore. He would be sure to forget the time, losing himself in something or other that came bound together in pages. I recovered in my uncle's outer office watching some sad goldfish in a bowl. Then I'd tire of waiting and wander downstairs and out to the corner to wait for my father's ugly, turtle-shaped, black-and-rust, 1947 Ford sedan.

When a half-hour or so went by and my mouth felt like I had chewed a wasp's nest, I began trudging up Eastern Avenue toward home, five miles away. And then I saw it coming. The Ford sedan crested the rise of the hill at a phenomenal speed, dust spewing from its tires. It was the *Green Hornet* and *The Shadow* and all the other programs we listened to on the radio. It squealed to a stop at the corner of Eastern and Burton, Dad's hands clenched at 2 and 10, waiting impatiently for the light while I ran back down Eastern hollering, "Here! Dad!"

Better than the Green Hornet. My hero. He took me out for an ice-cream cone to make up for the delay.

Now I stand behind him as he angles unsteadily up the steps. This will be the last time he drives his car, for we have agreed in a family meeting at Dad's house that he would not drive anymore. He gets more frail each week, it seems. In the past month he had fallen three times—once in his house during the night, once going down the three steps of his own house, and, most recently and tragically, a headlong fall into his cactus garden. My wife spent several hours with a tweezers picking cactus prickers out of his face and torso.

It is the way with all our heroes eventually. Finally, all they have to give is the precious legacy of the heart.

Only once in all history did a hero—of our faith—give us more than a legacy. Jesus gave a living presence. While we often struggle with caring for the infirmity of our elderly parents or friends in this life—making the tough choices, doing the tough actions—we are comforted by Jesus' legacy of love and life everlasting.

Luke 2:25–26, 28–29

Now there was a man in Jerusalem called Simeon, who was righteous and devout. He was waiting for the consolation of Israel, and the Holy Spirit was upon him. It had been revealed to him by the Holy Spirit that he would not die before he had seen the Lord's Christ.…Simeon took him in his arms and praised God, saying:

"Sovereign Lord, as you have promised,
you now dismiss your servant in peace."

Prayer

Lord, comfort us as we give comfort
to those whom we love
who are also aging.
Help us bear their infirmities
with them, to be kindly to them,
to support them in their final
steps through life's journey.
Amen.

THE COMFORTER:
IN GRIEF

W hen my children were young, they built tree forts and their laughter rang high in the blossoms of the apple tree like a bright pink, heavenly sound. They helped me in the garden when sun splashed all the mud puddles pale gold. They watched snow slide away from the green stalks of crocus and daffodils. We hiked through a North Carolina valley and they discovered a stand of lavender rhododendron that lit the edge of the forest.

They are grown now, and grown out of our house into loves and adventures of their own. So I sit at my desk in the study. I watch the winter ice that hangs from the eaves as if mother's Dutch cut-glass vases were fused in long, lacy streams. I remember my mother.

Grief, it seems, renders us comfortless. It cuts too deep and sharp a hole in our hearts. Nothing, it seems, can fill the loss. My mother's dying was sudden and yet it seemed to last forever. I admitted her to a hospital through the emergency room for the first time on Mother's Day, 1994. A cruel irony. What was first diagnosed as a bladder infection was found, through a series of re-admissions and tests, to be bladder cancer, and that of a particularly virulent sort. Chemotherapy and radiation, all those tricks of the medical trade to cheat death, ensued. I became more familiar with the hospital than my own home.

Then the last hospitalization, the long lapse into the long coma, the death watch, the decisions to be made, the countless hours at the bedside talking into the coma, kissing unresponsive lips, swabbing a mouth that heaved for every breath. And at last, the cruel mercy of her dying.

But that isn't how I remember my mother. Not at the bedside that November third, 1994, one day after my father's birthday. Truly, that moment is indelibly pressed —-into my mind. What I remember her for, however, is this.

I am sure that there are some mothers whose idea of heaven is simply a place where they won't have to cook anymore. Maybe they will be waited on more often than they were on earth; maybe their celestial bodies won't need the coarse grub that passes for food here. If the lion and the lamb lie down together, after all, won't the cow be safe? Or maybe we'll all be vegetarians. Plucking ceaselessly ripe, plump fruit in the new Eden. That would solve the problem.

Except for my mother. She would have wanted a wedding feast and she would have wanted to be at the very center of its preparation. One would think she would have had enough of it. As one of three daughters of a widow during the Great Depression, she chipped in to the family's meager resources by working at a bakery. Welfare assistance at that time consisted of a weekly gallon of milk obtained from the fire station. Nor did her financial status improve a great deal when she married my father, a young teacher with great skill at baseball and in the classroom but with a cruelly pinched salary. Yet, they hosted book clubs and occasionally a penniless student who needed a place to crash, and they fed all the guests lavishly.

My childhood memories focus often on the parties at our house—cakes and pies and assorted sweets for a room full of people. When I got older, I would sneak out of bed after the party and eat my fill. And there would be meals that would take one's breath away around that big old dining-room table. Still today, I have people remind me of those happy times spent in our living room or dining room, places of great laughter and gracious food.

There were certain events Mother insisted upon hosting. For example, the annual gathering of "the cousins" somehow squeezed into my parent's tiny condominium. Or New Year's Day, when the table would be laid out with a buffet of foods to which we helped ourselves during breaks in the Rose Bowl. But especially each of her children's—and their spouse's—birthdays. I can see that table spread out in my honor yet—I can nearly smell its rich scents. The Swiss steak piled high in layers on the platter. A half-dozen different vegetables, including the ones I liked but nobody else did—sweet potatoes and beets. It was a celebration to make your heart pound.

Often my wife asked Mom for recipes for a favorite dish. Only a few were ever written down, and these Mother modified to suit her own creative whimsy. When Pat asked Mom for a recipe for a certain cake once, it went something like…"A heaping cup of…a generous teaspoon of…" But it would never taste the same. Perhaps Mom's recipes went all the way back to those days when she worked in the bakery during the Depression for 12 cents an hour. She took something of infinitely more worth from that time than the wage. She took a spirit of celebration, a festivity, that enriched all who knew her. I don't know, of course, what kind, if any, dining will be done in heaven. But if it is, I know that heaven is a still brighter place by Mom's being there.

Therein lies the glory just on the other side of grief. In this life we cannot escape grief; in the eternal life it disappears from our vocabulary. Shortly before his death, Jesus told his disciples, "In my Father's house are many rooms; if it were not so, I would have told you. I am going there to prepare a place for you" (John 14:2). Jesus went there through the cross. All who come to the cross have room beyond grief built for them.

Isaiah 65:19

> I will rejoice over Jerusalem
> and take delight in my people;
> the sound of weeping and of crying
> will be heard in it no more.

Prayer

> In mansions of glory and endless delight,
> I'll ever adore Thee in heaven so bright;
> I'll sing with the glittering crown on my brow:
> If ever I loved Thee, my Jesus, 'tis now.
> Amen.

THE COMFORTER:
IN SUFFERING

Having raised four children, it sometimes seems to my wife and me that we have also raised fourscore pets. The feeble and strayed of the world have been carried to our door by little hands. "Dad, can we keep it?" became a regular plea.

Over the years we have had a series of birds to be nursed, of those eminently tired turtles that plod around in a cage for a while before being released in the nearby creek. We have had the goldfish gone gray and destined for the toilet ceremony, where the toddler waves bye-bye as mom or dad flushes. Hamsters and bunnies have had their time. And, like any family with a penchant toward pets, we have always had dogs we have loved and lived with, through all their doggy quirks and affliction.

Care, comfort, entertainment, even protection—they are all parts of the role pets play in our lives, maybe even bits of grace God sheds on our way. One example stands out in particular.

On June 8, 1986, my nephew, Johnny Timmerman, was born into a world of heart monitors, tubes, and other medical machinery that he would revisit many times during the following years.

John was born with a defect known as trisomy 22 syndrome. Medical people often refer to such children simply as a "syndrome baby." Most babies with trisomy 22 never survive pregnancy. The medical literature on the syndrome is so scant that we could find little on defining characteristics, expectations, and so forth. Those in the medical profession carefully avoided saying how long John would survive. The indications, however, were not at all hopeful. His infant body was limp one moment, rigid and contorted the next. But John was a survivor. One surgery followed another; one hurried trip to the emergency room after the other.

With care John learned to master first one skill and then another. He learned how to hold a utensil to feed himself, how to recognize some things, how to say a few basic words. But his muscular development was profoundly slowed. He would collapse limply when someone tried to lift him, his hands flailing uncontrollably. Still, there seemed to be more in this impish, bright-eyed child. His sense of humor was delightful. He would sneak off with a glove hanging from a coat pocket and hide, with a smile as wide as forever on his face.

Then this event happened, something that hadn't happened in all the world of human trying to this point, or all the best efforts of medicine or education.

One day, my sister-in-law was driving home when a sign caught her eye: *Equest Center for Therapeutic Riding.* Therapy through riding? When we have the best efforts of medicine and education? Nonetheless, my sister-in-law contacted the owners. After one visit, she signed John up for a program.

The first time he rode, John was balanced on the horse by a special pad with rings on the side to hold him in place. Sidewalkers, or guides, held him firmly on the horse. Then, gradually, John began to sit up on the horse, eventually alternating directions in which he sat in order to exercise different muscle groups. When John first started at the Equest Center he could not stand, even with help. He seemed destined to a lifetime in wheelchairs. Not long before he died, he rode a horse standing up on the saddle with sidewalker guides holding his hands.

From one point of view, it may seem very much like an act of faith. John had grown as he gained faith in his horse. So, too, does a believer grow as his or her faith in God develops. John's response was nothing short of a miracle. We never expected him to live as long as he did (he died in 2006), but his life was marked by joy.

What comfort do we find during the sufferings that torment our daily lives? I think my nephew provides an answer. Remember that he never would have made it to the saddle of his horse, nor the first few steps around the ring, nor the moment when he stood proudly on the horse's back, without those two sidewalkers. They were his guides and security. He was never totally alone.

In a sense, each of us, in times of illness or in times of health, have the sidewalker of the Holy Spirit. With that guide we are directed, and cannot stumble out of God's will. In those moments when illness—physical or psychological—stretches us on a bed of pain, then, too, our Sidewalker is with us.

The cross on Calvary cut a crosswise link between us and the throne of the Father. Therein lies our consolation in illness—even in death.

John 17:11

"I will remain in the world no longer, but they are still in the world, and I am coming to you. Holy Father, protect them by the power of your name—the name you gave me—so that they may be one as we are one."

Prayer

So often when illness strikes, Lord,
I feel isolated. It is not a happy state,
especially when it lingers.
May I feel you then on each side of me,
holding my hand,
guiding me.
Amen.

Day Fifteen

Eternal Life

I sometimes think of eternal life as a kind of thing, some kind of event that happens after death. Then I get confused. Does it happen to me? Do I just change so that one minute I am in this world of time and the next I am in a world where time has little meaning? Eternal—hard to get a grip on that here on earth.

And more. In Michigan, winters seem to last forever. Those summer days pass in a blink. Yet summer days have so much light, how can they seem to pass so quickly—as if hours started speeding up around early May? Will eternity have seasons? Do I get to choose what part I'll live in?

When my mind acts like that, I lean back and say to myself, "You know, it really doesn't matter one bit." Why not? Philosophers and theologians have speculated on eternal life since ancient times. Sometimes I read a few of those books and think that maybe I should be spending more attention on it. After all, I'll be spending a long time there.

But then I realize that I'm misunderstanding eternal life altogether. Eternal life isn't some "it," nor a "thing." Eternal life, the Bible clearly tells me, is being with Jesus. And, if this is the case, if the Bible is true—and I find no good internal evidence to doubt that it is—a remarkable, time-shattering fact appears. Eternal life is present with me now.

In John's first epistle, he makes this undeniably clear. Speaking of the testimony of God about Jesus, John writes, "And this is the testimony: God has given us eternal life, and his life is in his Son" (5:11). Moreover, John adds that "We are in him who is true—even in his Son Jesus Christ. He is the true God and eternal life" (5:20). The startling fact is that as we are in Jesus, we are in God and we are in eternal life. Eternal life is our true state of being, our true home, even now.

The Gospel of John, sometimes called the "Gospel of Light" since it reveals the Light of the World and is the light to our path, emphasizes our state in eternal life as a major theme. The familiar John 3:16 states: "For God so loved the world that he gave his one and only Son, that whoever believes in him shall not perish but have eternal life." The theme from the epistle is amplified here; when we believe in Jesus, we *have* eternal life. John states it slightly differently in 17:3. Here Jesus is praying to his father: "Now this is eternal life: that they may know you, the only true God, and Jesus Christ, whom you have sent." Eternal life *is* knowing Jesus. That is something we experience now.

Nonetheless, as Saint Paul said, I am well aware that in this life "I know in part; then I shall know fully..." (1 Corinthians 13:12). Eternal life will spring joy and surprises beyond human comprehension or expectation.

Recently I received a letter that seems to me an interesting document on this very subject. It was written by a young lady who had suffered much in her brief life, and whose suffering frequently made her feel of little worth in the eyes of God and humanity. But she knew powerfully that Jesus loved her, and that fact led to this affirmation of her eternal life:

> I feel like I'll get into heaven. But I'll have to sneak through a little crack in the back door. Even then I'll have to run hard because some angel might be there, ready to stomp me like a bug. "You don't belong." I'll sneak then through the long-bladed grass like a scared rabbit—until I find a patch of brush where I can rest and ask: "Is this me? And is this really me? And am I really here? But why?" Maybe it is enough to eat clover for the wedding feast.

Maybe, just maybe, this is one of the richest affirmations of eternal life I have ever read. Out of great trial, she carved a rock-hard belief that, no matter what, she stood with her Redeemer now and for eternity. Sometimes pure joy lies in eating clover at the wedding feast.

Job 19:25–27

I know that my Redeemer lives,
    and that in the end he will stand upon the earth.
And after my skin has been destroyed,
    yet in my flesh I will see God;
I myself will see him
    with my own eyes—I, and not another.
    How my heart yearns within me!

Prayer

At all times, and in all suffering,
I cling to that assertion of Job—
"I know that my Redeemer lives."
If you have redeemed me, Jesus,
I am never apart from you.
Bless me with your comfort.
Quiet my heart, still my mind.
Whatever discomforts me
I hand over to you,
trusting in your good and perfect love.
Amen.

Day Sixteen

THE BREAD OF LIFE: BROKEN FOR YOU

While they were eating, Jesus took bread, gave thanks and broke it, and gave it to his disciples, saying, "Take and eat; this is my body" (Matthew 26:26).

It is, by all measure, one of the most intimate moments in the New Testament. Jesus and the disciples recline in a circle in the upper room. Evening light falls through the window. It is warm up here, the air still close at the end of the day. And they are all tired on this Passover.

Yet, they are together. The inner core of Jesus' closest disciples. Even Judas is there, identified now as a traitor. A shiver of fear must have spiked coldly through Judas. He knows. Did the other disciples understand, or even suspect? Judas knew the other side.

Only days before, Jesus had made his triumphal entry into Jerusalem. From the moment he arrived, he began teaching in the temple. Crowds swarmed. This was Jesus' house now. The simple parables he taught were not rigid codes, not the chief priests' way. He told stories, the people listened, and they hungered for more.

For the Jewish leaders it could not have come at a worse time. The high and holy day of the Passover quickly drew near, and they were losing control. They looked for "some way to get rid of Jesus" (Luke 22:2), to re-establish their proper authority over custom and tradition. Who dared, however? Look at the crowds. How could anyone break through them to the object of their attention and adoration and "get rid of Jesus"?

In the same way that Satan insinuated his way into Eden, turning the world upside down, he enters here in what will turn the world right side up. Necessarily, the bread had to be broken. At the moment, however, the ancient foe saw the opportunity—and seized it. He entered Judas, called Iscariot, one of the twelve.

Judas appears never to have been at the forefront of the disciples. Indeed, his name always appears last in the list, often with the stigma of a term like "who became a traitor" (Luke 6:16) following his name. This, however, is due to the fact that the gospels were written long after the events were recorded. Among the disciples Judas held the position of treasurer, although John adds that he was a thief (12:6), raising suspicion that he pilfered money from the funds donated to Jesus' ministry. Judas was, we might say, predisposed to his act of betrayal.

Further evidence from Scripture may be tallied against Judas. He was a greedy man. He criticizes Mary's anointing of Jesus' feet with the precious ointment. Remember Jesus' reply? "Leave her alone…it was intended that she should save this perfume for the day of my burial. You will always have the poor among you, but you will not always have me" (John 12:7–8). Jesus rebuked Judas, knowing full well that Judas wanted the money for himself. Judas was overripe fruit for Satan to worm his way into and use as he wished. There never was a healthy core to the man.

In all this, however, we remember that Judas was nothing more than a pawn when he crept out to the chief priests on the sly and told them he had a plan to sell out Jesus. It was Satan in him. Jesus fully knew that plan and his ancient foe. Judas' purpose among the disciples was to betray Jesus, to break the master's body in the same way the bread was broken. Jesus knew the betrayer of his life sat, for the last time, at the table breaking bread with him.

This is the close of Jesus' ministry—that precious, intimate moment with the eleven who loved him. The one who was to betray him had slipped out into the night to do his dirty work.

In one of those moments of unsurpassed, heart-wrenching beauty, however, when all the Scripture makes perfect sense and we see the wholeness, the power, and completion of our Lord's work on earth, we understand that this is not the final moment. When Satan darkened

Eden, God had a plan for the world's restoration. When Satan entered Judas, God enacted that very plan. But one additional, intervening step occurred in the enactment. We cannot forget that before he even started his ministry as the Messiah, Jesus met Satan head-on in a temptation of such proportions that it made Judas a minor cog in God's design.

To prepare for his ministry, Jesus was led by the Spirit into the wilderness. For forty days he fasted. The numerical count in itself is significant, used throughout Scripture as a full and thorough completion of a human ordeal. During the great flood of Noah, rain fell for forty days and nights, signifying the complete inundation of the earth. In the desert the Israelites ate manna for forty years, signifying God's complete control and care for them. After his crucifixion, Jesus appeared to the disciples for a period of forty days before he ascended into heaven, signifying his presence with them as resurrected Lord. And he fasted forty days in the wilderness when Satan tempted him.

Jesus was hungry. Satan's first temptation, understandably, was to that hunger. He offered bread. The irony is heartbreaking. Satan offered bread to the One who is the Bread of Life. If Jesus had accepted it, however, he would no longer be the Bread of Life to us. He would merely be like Judas, one who gobbled up the bread and fled into the darkness, all hope gone. But Jesus responds, "It is written: 'Man does not live on bread alone, but on every word that comes from the mouth of God'" (Matthew 4:4).

That too is the Bread of Life to us—to feed ourselves on the word of God. So Jesus did on the very night he was betrayed, when the traitor dipped bread with him in the bowl. What separates us from Judas? Not that we will never do anything wrong; not that we will never commit our own betrayals. Rather, unlike Judas, we believe that Jesus is the Bread of Life, broken for us, that we might dwell by his side forever.

Psalm 105:40

They asked, and he brought them quail
And satisfied them with the bread of heaven.

Prayer

Lord, you are the bread of Life,
without which my days would be famine,
my spirit ever hungry.
It is your body, broken for me,
that I pray for in my body,
my thinking, my talking, my very life.
Amen.

Day Seventeen

THE BREAD OF LIFE:
OUR ESSENTIAL NUTRIENT

B read was the essential staple in Jewish communities. Families started the day early with a simple meal of bread. Often with something like olives, or cheese, or some dried fruit on it. If there had been something like a government agency of required foods in ancient Israel, bread would have topped the list. Often the bread itself was purchased in the communal market, where the town baker baked the loaves in an oven overnight.

Since it was the staple of life, however, many undertook the cooking in their own domed ovens. They mixed flour from their hand mills with water, leavened the loaf with a piece of the previous day's bread, and left it by the fire until the yeast from the old piece leavened the entire loaf. When ready, it was baked in the oven, or it was simply left on a rack by the fire to bake. Daily bread—it was the essential food among God's chosen people.

So essential that the lack of bread constituted a dire threat to the people. Perhaps the clearest example of this lies in the manna provided to the Israelites. This always fractious people; over a million of them, groused about the lack of bread. Some wanted to cut out and go back to Egypt. Any life, even slavery they thought, was better than this life. Then those heavenly flakes, newly fallen like grace each morning, floated before them. Perhaps it was in recollection of just this event that Isaiah, in his portrait of the Messiah's reign, prophesied that "The cowering prisoners will be set free; / they will not die in the dungeon, / nor will they lack bread" (51:14). Conversely, the author of Lamentations paints an altogether bleak portrait of people lacking the life-giving bread. In the second chapter, he sees children starving in their mother's arms, crying out for bread (see 2:11–12). The heart-wrenching portrait is repeated in successive chapters, drawing to mind pictures of the starving and begging children around our world today. They cry out for bread. They cry out for the living bread.

From the ancient world to our own time, the cry goes out—give us bread to eat.

In the remarkable intimacy that Jesus shared with his fellow humans, he knew full well that cry. In his pointed sermon beginning with the beatitudes, Jesus includes his lesson on the simplicity of prayer. In that context, he offers the familiar "Jesus prayer"—sharp, to the point, unadorned as he said by "babbling like pagans." One of the essentials in his teaching prayer strikes the heart of all humanity: "Give us today our daily bread" (Matthew 6:11). Many words have been written on just that line, many books on the urgent simplicity of Jesus' prayer. The inescapable fact, however, is that Jesus directs us away from the luxuries and pretenses of our lives and back to the fundamentals—Give us this day our daily bread.

The prayer holds no less now than it did at Jesus' time. But what is this bread? Surely, it is, at one level, our fundamental need for physical nourishment. We pray to the Father for that, and we are grateful that he provides it. But Jesus certainly took this a step further.

We turn to another scene. This time crowds follow Jesus, longing to hear his teaching and receive his healing. They find him by the Sea of Galilee. He has just recently fed the crowd of five thousand by the miracle of the loaves and fishes. Did the crowd come looking for more miraculous signs? Jesus anticipates them, "Do not work for food that spoils, but for food that endures to eternal life, which the Son of Man will give you" (John 6:27). These are mysterious words. Carefully, Jesus explains: "I tell you the truth, it is not Moses who has given you the bread from heaven, but it is my Father who gives you the true bread from heaven. For the bread of God is he who comes down from heaven and gives life to the world" (John 6:32–33). Finally and frankly, Jesus tells them, "I am the bread of life" (6:48). And he adds—I imagine to their astonishment and bewilderment—that "I am the living bread that came down from heaven. If anyone eats of this bread, he will live forever. This bread is my flesh, which I will give for the life of the world" (6:51).

Return for a moment to that upper room where Jesus broke bread with his disciples. Did everything begin to fall in place for them? Or for us? Jesus took bread, gave thanks, and broke it. Then he said, "This is my body given for you; do this in remembrance of me" (Luke 22:19). This bread is now our daily nourishment, the one thing we cannot live without. Jesus' sacrifice, broken and given to us, is necessary now, but also seals our fellowship with him to all eternity.

Exodus 16:31–32

The people of Israel called the bread manna. It was white like coriander seed and tasted like wafers make with honey. Moses said, "This is what the LORD has commanded: 'Take an omer of manna and keep it for the generations to come, so they can see the bread I gave you to eat in the desert when I brought you out of Egypt.'"

Prayer

Lord, as you supplied daily manna
to the Israelites in exile,
so I ask you to nurture me with your daily bread—
the Living Bread, broken for me
that I might live with you always.
Amen.

Day Eighteen

THE TRUE VINE:
OUR PERSONAL GOD

When I consider some of the major world religions today, I am struck by how remote their gods are. For example, Confucianism, adhered to by millions of people, dispenses with a god altogether. Confucius lived about five hundred years before Jesus, and his teachings were collected by his disciples in the *Analects*. Basically, the work tells one how to live a serene and ethical life. And that is all. Hinduism, on the other hand, also a religion with millions of adherents, features so many gods and variations of divinities that one can hardly keep them all straight. Among these Eastern variations, perhaps the most perplexing is Buddhism, which holds that as one extinguishes the self and self-desire, one attains spiritual enlightenment.

But one does not have to traverse the religions of foreign lands to locate such impersonal "gods." In the Western world, humans have also succeeded in stripping their lives of the divine. They either claim there is no divine beyond this life at all, or they lose themselves in faddish, self-help meditations, cults, and spiritualism. In all the variations, such people deny the presence of a Savior, the one true God, in their lives here and now.

I am amazed how often Jesus refers to the most common tasks and affairs of humanity. He affirms his role as God with us—Immanuel. Jesus' teaching examples are often simple, yet they cut through the flurry of issues to the very heart of truth. Would you talk about who gives the most to the kingdom? Let's consider the widow's mite. Would you discuss the sin of drunkenness? Let's remember the prodigal son who came home. Do you have great needs? Let's consider the sparrow. So it is with the names Jesus gives himself; they speak of everyday realities.

Why is this? Why does Jesus identify himself in the simple terms of common, daily life?

Jesus is not foremost a subject for theologians; he is foremost a man among men, the divine touch on the humblest stations of humanity, the light of God in the smallest, most dismal corner of life. Jesus lives theology in the church of daily life. He is not a rabbi of the synagogue; he is Rabboni among the people.

Some titles of Jesus bespeak his great glory. *Bright Morning Star* is a majestic name, thundering across the vast stretches of spiritual night in unalterable light. *Alpha and Omega* testifies to the perfect divinity of Jesus; he is the One who began all that is, and he is the One in whom all is fulfilled. But then we have a name like the *True Vine*, and we see Jesus once again among us.

"I am the true vine...you are the branches," Jesus says to his disciples (John 15:1, 5). But why the vine? It is easy for us to picture the cornerstone of a building, and when Jesus says he is the cornerstone of the church, we immediately intuit that our faith is built on him. But the vine? Did he choose this image because wine was a communal drink for mealtimes and the passing of the cup suggested unity?

Israel, God's chosen nation, often is spoken of in the Old Testament as a vine. Several times, Ezekiel describes Israel as a once splendid vine now grown useless and good for nothing (see Ezekiel 15:1–8; 19:10–14). To bear fruit, vineyards must be tended carefully. Ezekiel shows that, despite God's tender care, Israel willfully allows itself to sprawl into ruin. Vines need support; without such their fruit rots and disease attacks. Ruin is also the subject of Isaiah's parable (see Isaiah 5:1–7). And Jeremiah (2:21) states it more directly:

> "I had planted you like a choice vine,
>   of sound and reliable stock.
> How then have you turned against me
>   into a corrupt, wild vine?"

Jesus speaks in John 15 about his nature as the True Vine, describing himself as a new vine from which the true church may be built. As branches of the vine, we take our lives by being grafted into him. This graft is made and nourished, says Jesus, by the Father, the vinedresser.

This name for Jesus, with its image of us being grafted into him, offers great security. As his life pours into us, the grafted branches, we become one with him, the main vine. What is the vine without its fruit-bearing branches? Who can say where the branch begins and the vine ends? This name emphasizes our oneness, our unity, with Jesus in much the same way that the passing of the cup at his Last Supper emphasized Jesus' unity with his disciples.

I think again of those religions with remote, dispassionate, uncaring gods. Which god ever offered to reach down into the world's dusty streets and offer to be human? And which not only offered, but was able, to graft us into him to become sons and daughters of the most high God?

John 15:5–8

"I am the vine; you are the branches. If a man remains in me and I in him, he will bear much fruit; apart from me you can do nothing. If anyone does not remain in me, he is like a branch that is thrown away and withers; such branches are picked up...and burned. If you remain in me and my words remain in you, ask whatever you wish, and it will be given you. This is to my Father's glory, that you bear much fruit, showing yourselves to be my disciples."

Prayer

This is the calling I want to follow:
to be grafted into you, Lord, the True Vine.
Then, help me bear fruit,
to reach the lost and wandering,
those twisted by deceits,
and with the help of the Holy Spirit,
lead them to your safe side also.
Amen.

Day Nineteen

THE TRUE VINE: SHED FOR YOU

Wine, like bread, was a common staple in the Jewish community. In the culture of Jesus' time, this use of wine as a common drink was understandable. Often the water sources were polluted by animal use. Cisterns, used to collect water that ran off the rooftops, also collected the debris that came with it. It might do for bathing, but one wouldn't want to drink too much of it. Consequently, vineyards were an important industry, and, in fact, nearly every settled Jew wanted a small trellised vine of his own near his home.

When a landowner decided to raise a commercial vineyard, it was often a painstaking and expensive project. Jesus' allusion to the wealthy owner of the vineyard in his parable would immediately have been understood by his listeners. The vineyard was built on a hill slope to promote good drainage; the plants set in rows terraced by stones. Such vineyards may still be seen today. While varieties of grapes were left to sprawl, the more careful owners supported the vines on forked sticks, forming a rude but effective trellis.

During the August to September harvest, some grapes were laid out to dry for raisins but most were destined for the winepress. This was simply a large cistern, cut out of rock with a drainage hole in the bottom, and large enough for several people at a time to gather in the press and tread the grapes. It was a communal time, full of festivity and good cheer. After the juice fermented for about six weeks, allowing the *lees,* or sediment, to separate, it was bottled and sealed with clay.

Lest we think that all this preparation and labor was only a commercial process, however, we should remember that the grapes and wine bore religious significance for the Israelites. For example, in Psalm 80:14–15, Asaph compares Israel to the vineyard and prays:

> Return to us, O God Almighty!
> Look down from heaven and see!
> Watch over this vine,
> the root your right hand has planted,
> the son you have raised up for yourself.

A similar passage appears in Isaiah 5:1–5. On the one hand, such figures are immensely comforting. We live in the gentle touch of the great vinedresser, the one who guides and nurtures our lives. The very real issue arises, however, that sometimes for individual health pruning must occur, and that sometimes for communal health an entire vine must be ripped out and destroyed. These are acts of sacrifice for welfare and health.

They also help us understand what happened in the upper room during the Passover meal, when Jesus said to his disciples, as he held up the cup of wine, "Drink from it, all of you. This is my blood of the covenant, which is poured out for many for the forgiveness of sins. I tell you, I will not drink of this fruit of the vine from now on until that day when I drink it anew with you in my Father's kingdom" (Matthew 26:27–29). Utterly mystifying words, it seems. Unless we remember that wine was the life-giving, "safe" drink of the time. Unless we understand that it was a communal drink and now Jesus announces a new "covenant" of those who believe in him and are thereby cleansed by his blood.

The gracious reality of this life-changing gift became powerfully real for me during one Good Friday worship service. It is the custom of my congregation to meet to celebrate the Lord's Supper. The lights are dimmed as we enter the sanctuary from the evening's twilight. One has a sense of the presence of the Lord, that this is a holy place where Jesus is with us "even to the ends of the earth." A light falls on the cross, draped in purple. A large glass bowl of crystal-clear water stands before the altar. Just prior to the partaking of holy Communion, slips of paper are distributed throughout the congregation. The paper feels unusual, its texture slightly grainy. This is not ordinary paper. When we are asked to use the red pens in the pew racks, the words seem to bleed onto the paper, as if they are hurting it. We are asked to write down our sins. It hurts from inside us; it bleeds onto the paper. We are asked to fold them.

The slip of paper trembles in my hand. I am grateful no one else can see what is written there. No one?

Row by row, we come forward to take Communion. The bread of his body, broken for me. The wine of his blood, poured out for me. As people come forward, they drop their slips of paper into the bowl. An elder stirs them with a wooden spoon. It almost looks like the upright of a cross. But as he stirs, the paper dissolves. It disappears. No matter how much is put in the bowl, the paper disappears. As far as the east is from the west. The water takes on a pinkish tint.

My pew stands. We inch forward toward the altar. No one hurries. I stand by the bowl. The water is red now, nearly scarlet. There is not a trace of paper, none of those words or deeds, in it. Hand trembling, I drop my paper in, watch it swirl into the spoon's turning, its words disappearing into the red flow. I approach the Communion table.

"This is my blood for the covenant, which is poured out for many for the forgiveness of sins."

I have drunk the wine of that covenant. I am forgiven. I am made new.

Psalm 103:11–12

For as high as the heavens are above the earth,
    so great is his love for those who fear him;
as far as the east is from the west,
    so far has he removed our transgressions from us.

Prayer

Sadness mingles with joy, Jesus.
My transgressions grieve me.
Yet, I am struck with wondrous joy
that you have taken them upon you,
and in one miraculous moment
dissolved them in your grace.
Amen.

Day Twenty

THE TEMPLE

The last time I counted, I had eighty-one roses in separate gardens around my house. Not an extravagant number, for I know people who have hundreds. But even eighty-one roses require an inordinate amount of care.

Are they worth it? Every time I catch my wife splashing barefoot through the dewy grass to pick a bouquet they are. Every time I lean over, cup the petals, and inhale the fragrance they are.

Is it too much to imagine that our sacrifice of praise raised in the temple of our churches, or the temple of our lives, is like a sweet incense before God? And that, like the gardener, God bends over us to receive that gift of praise and to bestow his blessing in turn?

The burning of fragrant incense was an essential part of the Old Testament church from its earliest days. The dramatic change to the New Testament of course is the Incarnation—the Immanuel or "God with us." Through Jesus, God is in our very midst. The fragrant offering we present is nothing less and no more than our very lives. Paul wrote to the Ephesians: "Be imitators of God, therefore, as dearly loved children and live a life of love, just as Christ loved us and gave himself up for us as a fragrant offering and sacrifice to God" (5:1–2).

Two implications arise from this passage that exhort us to be imitators of Christ and to make our lives a fragrant offering to him. First, we ourselves are a temple where Jesus takes residence. In Paul's letters, this theme beats like lifeblood behind his other precepts. In 1 Corinthians 3:16 he writes, "Don't you know that you yourselves are God's temple and that God's Spirit lives in you?" Variations of the verse appear in many other passages, but the implication in each is clear—our very lives, our very being, constitute God's temple.

A second implication is that the temple was and continues to be a place where others come to be ministered to, renewed, and illuminated. In his second letter to the Corinthians, Paul again writes of the Christian life being like a fragrant offering: "For we are to God the aroma of Christ among those who are being saved and those who are perishing" (2:15). Then Paul changes his metaphor slightly: "You show that you are a letter from Christ, the result of our ministry, written not with ink but with the Spirit of the living God, not on tablets of stone but on tablets of human hearts" (3:3). Never is the task of the believer to bottle up the Spirit in his or her own temple. Offering our lives like incense is only half of the equation. The other half is the question, "Now what do we do with our lives?"

The answer comes from the very One to whom we make the offering of our lives. Jesus is our final and authoritative temple. Just as the Old Testament temple was said to hold the glory of God, Jesus holds the glory of our salvation. In the same passage in Matthew where Jesus declares himself Lord of the Sabbath, he adds, "I tell you that one greater than the temple is here" (12:6). Most powerful of all, however, were Jesus' challenging words to the Jews after he cleared the moneychangers from the temple. When the Jews demanded under what authority he did this, Jesus responded, "Destroy this temple, and I will raise it again in three days" (John 2:19).

The Jews saw only the physical building, forty-six years in the making. It was a strong and intricate building, the very pride of their nation. But Jesus was looking beyond that temple. He saw where this early action in his ministry was leading him. It ended at the cross, when the temple veil was torn in two and when the temple of the Son of God was offered before the Father for our forgiveness.

Yes, and that temple was raised up in three days. Now that new temple is the fellowship of believers with their risen Lord.

Isaiah 43:18–19

"Forget the former things;
    do not dwell on the past.
See, I am doing a new thing!
    Now it springs up; do you not perceive it?
I am making a way in the desert
    and streams in the wasteland."

Prayer

Dear Lord, in the presence of your temple
I bow down before you.
Accept my life as an offering of praise,
redeemed by your blood, Lord.
Do a new thing in me;
Help me forget the former things;
let my life be alive in your life.
Amen.

Day Twenty-One

THE LAW

During this Lenten season we turn our thoughts to Jesus' grace, freely given. It might seem odd, then, to consider him as the fulfillment of the Law. But that is exactly how Jesus sees himself, and we cannot avoid speaking of the Law when we speak of grace.

Matthew 5 records Jesus' Sermon on the Mount, a beautiful parallel to God's revelation to Moses on the mount at Horeb. In the crowd listening to Jesus stood people who had put the Law above all things—above grace, above love. They approached the Mosaic Law with rigid legalism that froze human relations. Now Jesus stood before them as the Lord of grace and love, the healer of broken relationships, and said, "Do not think that I have come to abolish the Law or the Prophets; I have not come to abolish them but to fulfill them" (Matthew 5:17). The Law is now fulfilled in grace. How do we understand Jesus as the Law?

Like the Pharisees, we often think of laws in terms of restrictions. Especially in the United States, perhaps, where the Constitution was written to protect individual freedoms, we become suspicious of anything that may limit those freedoms. In such a climate of thought, which views additional laws as something like a dark cloud on a distant horizon that threatens the sunny brightness of individual freedom, we find it hard to conceive of law itself as a good and positive thing. Yet, we have to admit that the constitutional basis for our law is also at once the basis for our freedom, that without law we would have mere anarchy, and that in the absence of law, we would have a kind of social reversion where only the strong survive, feeding off the weaker members of society. Even granting that, however, is it possible to see a system of law not just as a protector of freedom, not just as an agenda for social order, but also—shockingly—as a living relationship of loving closeness?

That is precisely the state between God's laws and us. Rather than just restrictive rules of what we should not do, God's law is liberating and prescriptive of a loving relationship. Chapters 8 and 9 of Nehemiah, where Ezra reads the long-lost law, are revealing. Some commentators have it that anticipation was high among the Israelites when Ezra called them to the reading of God's law. People flowed into Jerusalem from outlying villages. They gathered before dawn, standing nearly shoulder to shoulder in the large open square by the Water Gate. Then, as the first orange of the sun appeared, the people called out for Ezra and the law of the Lord. A platform had been constructed high above the people. Followed by thirteen chief priests, Ezra carried the Book of the Law before him, ascended the platform, and began reading. For six straight hours he read, but for these people it was no drudgery. They "lifted their hands and responded, 'Amen! Amen!'" Then they bowed to the ground and worshiped God. But there is one little catch here: "Then they bowed down and worshiped the LORD *with their faces to the ground*" [emphasis mine] (8:6).

This is the Jewish prostration, the attitude of mourning. If they bowed in respect to the awesome God, they fell to the ground in acknowledgment of how far they had fallen short of his law. This is not hard for us to understand. Our first encounter with any law is either a sudden denial or a sudden acknowledgment of our wrongdoing.

Nehemiah and Ezra, however, saw a larger picture: This law is for your protection. Do not grieve. Celebrate the fact that you have a God who loves you and gives you these laws for your protection. They encourage the people to prepare a feast of celebration for "This day is sacred to our Lord. Do not grieve, for the joy of the LORD is your strength" (Nehemiah 8:10).

The Israelites learned once again that the law of the Lord was their delight. As the author of Psalm 119, a psalm praising God's law, put it: "The earth is filled with your love, O LORD; / teach me your decrees" (119:64). God's law is a revelation of his love, a means for maintaining a close walk with him on this earth.

Nothing could be more appropriate than that Jesus calls himself the fulfillment of the Law and the Prophets. Yes, he fulfilled all that the prophets foresaw about the coming Messiah. But also, as the embodiment of God's love and grace, he fulfilled every one of God's laws so that we might have a loving relationship with him.

Deuteronomy 6:4–5

Hear, O Israel: The LORD our God, the LORD is one. Love the LORD your God with all your heart and with all your soul and with all your strength.

Prayer

Thank you, Lord Jesus, for fulfilling the Law.
You gave yourself, the perfect atonement,
for all my sins.
You let me walk in grace and love,
freed from the misery of guilt and shame.
You are my Lord, my perfect Law.
Amen.

THE LIVING WATER

A s in Jesus' day, the modern country of Israel is a paradox of geography and climates. In the northern highland regions, adequate rains support agriculture—vineyards, olive groves, farmlands. Tributaries of highland streams flow together into the vast, clear waters of the Sea of Galilee. Today fishermen still can net their catch, precisely as Simon Peter did.

Then the hilly highlands fall away to rough rock escarpments, and here the rains seem to end. The dry land sucks up what little rain does fall. It is a land for goats and sheep to forage. To live there, the Israelites had to know where the pools and springs were. Sometimes they dug wells into the stony ground and for long months were dependent on these for the water without which they could not live. To the east of this region flowed the Jordan River, winding its slow track to the south from the Sea of Galilee, becoming ever more shallow and narrow and sediment-polluted with each mile.

Finally, there was the wasteland, the Negev Desert. I find it hard to understand all the wars the Old Testament Jews waged over this forsaken territory as they battled to drive their enemies back and to reinforce their southern borders. At times more blood than rain fell on its eerie wastes. A land of weirdly sculpted rocks, cliffs chiseled by wind and blowing sand, colors blending to tan and white and gray—it was the wasteland. And east and north of it, the last drops of the Jordan River fell into the Dead Sea, its waters so saline from the sun's work that it could support no life whatsoever. A bitter counterpart to the living waters of Galilee far to the north, where fish teemed and olive groves clung to its banks.

If the people of the Old Testament were brutally aware of the distinctions—life and death depended on them—so, too, were the people of Jesus' time. Water was still the precious commodity. Constant replenishment was necessary, but the reserves always seemed so low and so precious.

That fact is hard for us to wrap our minds around. If water is a necessary commodity for us too, it is easily obtainable. We turn a faucet at a sink. We tap power equipment into underground cisterns or wells. We purchase "designer" water in one-liter bottles at prices nearly as high as a gallon of gasoline.

We appreciate water the most in the horror of its absence. In 1922, shortly after World War I, T. S. Eliot wrote a poem, "The Waste Land," that would endure as one of the most famous works of our century. In it, Eliot claims that we have made a spiritual wasteland of our own lives, not unlike the physical wasteland of any desert region. But we have brought it upon ourselves. We have sought instant gratification rather than patient seeking; we have sought the momentary pleasures of lust rather than the committed promises of love. Our desert is one of the spirit. We wander lost and alone in it and can hardly hear the very sound of water.

It would be another five years, on July 27, 1927, that Eliot would find his source of living water when he was baptized into the Anglican Church.

Nearly two thousand years before "The Waste Land," however, Jesus had an answer for those wandering in a spiritual wasteland. In chapter 5, Matthew records Jesus' sermon on his mountain, the words commonly called the "Beatitudes," or "Blessings." In verse six, he utters one of the most perplexing: "Blessed are those who hunger and thirst for righteousness, for they will be filled" (5:6). The paradox of this beatitude, like all the others, is that it mixes a concrete, human experience with a divine relationship. I do not think Jesus is telling us to enter a relentless fast, wasting away until filled with a vision of his glory—although for some people that might be part of it. Rather, I think he tells us to hunger and thirst for a living relationship with him. As T. S. Eliot came to learn, only by that can we be filled. Only by the Living Water can our thirst for righteousness be satisfied.

Lent is marked by nothing quite so much as this hunger and thirst to see Jesus more clearly and to draw closer to him. We start that now—thirsting for God in a spiritually dry, arid, and unfulfilling land. Sometimes it is the landscape of our own souls.

Isaiah 66:12–13

For this is what the LORD says:
"I will extend peace to her like a river,
and the wealth of the nations like a flooding stream;
you will nurse and be carried on her arm
and dandled on her knees.
As a mother comforts her child,
so I will comfort you;
and you will be comforted over Jerusalem.

Prayer

Jesus my Lord—
Lord of heaven and of earth,
Lord of my life—
wash me with your comforting grace,
I pray.
Let it be like a refreshing stream,
a streak of blue sky that the sun plays in,
a newness of answers
for the never-ending why,
hope that beats back the shadows.
Amen.

Day Twenty-Three

THE LIVING WATER: DRINK FROM THE WELL

From time to time quiet little dramas unfold in the gospel accounts that tell us much about our Savior. We often tend to focus on those mountaintop stories—the Sermon on the Mount, the Passover Feast on the mountain by the Sea of Galilee where Jesus fed five thousand people with five loaves of bread and two small fish. Such passages resonate with the majesty of the Lord of the mountains. So, too, perhaps, we think of the triumphant entry from the hills above Jerusalem, the Mount of Olives agony, and, especially at Lent, the death on the Mount called Golgotha. Such scenes rivet our attention. Those quieter passages, however, bring Jesus into *our* reality as our human teacher and friend. As we read Scripture carefully, dozens of these scenes leak out through the larger conflicts and dramas. Picture Jesus taking little children on his lap and playing with them in the Galilean dust. Picture Jesus walking and talking with his disciples on the road to Bethany, where Jesus would raise Lazarus from the dead just days before he suffered his own death. Picture his tender restoration of Peter after Peter's denial.

These smaller dramas are important to me. How I would have loved to play in Jesus' arms as a little child. How I would have loved to walk with Jesus to Bethany, comrades along the road. Especially, like Peter after his denial, I long to hear Jesus' words of love and affirmation. I, too, can deny him so quickly and easily. Like an autumn leaf, I separate and drift from the root of David. I need Jesus' affirmation to Peter to affirm his love for me.

In one sense, Jesus' primary message is also simple and direct: "For God so loved the world that he gave his one and only Son, that whoever believes in him shall not perish but have eternal life" (John 3:16). That simple message would be the heart of Jesus' life and ministry. People thronged to him to be baptized. This caught the attention of those nervous little Pharisees, ever alert for any legal infraction. Consequently, Jesus left Judea for Galilee.

About noon of one day, Jesus was traveling, hot and tired, through Samaria when he came across the village of Sychar. Like all small communities, Sychar grew around a dependable water supply. This one happened to be the well that Jacob had given to Joseph. It was a deep well (when cleaned out in an excavation in 1935, it measured 138 feet deep), sufficient for the village and its livestock. While Jesus' disciples went into the town to purchase supplies, Jesus rested by the well.

At that moment a Samaritan woman walked out to draw water. I wonder if she hesitated when she saw the stranger by the well. Surely she perceived that he was a Jew, and surely she knew of the ancient antagonism between Jews and Samaritans. But this was, after all, the village well, and she needed water.

Then things fell apart.

When she approached, Jesus asked her to give him a drink. It would be one thing to draw her water in her routine way and escape to her routine life. But this Jew by the well asked for a drink, and everyone knew that Jews did not touch anything having to do with Samaritans. She protested. It's a wonder she didn't run away.

Here in this little moment of human reality and spiritual drama, we find the fundamental issue we all confront. Jesus had a physical need, very real and urgent. The woman had a spiritual need, just as real and urgent. "If you knew the gift of God and who it is that asks you for a drink," Jesus says to her, "you would have asked him and he would have given you living water" (John 4:10). The interesting thing in Jesus' response is that he speaks to her need. He does not put on some dazzling miracle show—as he could have done. No water from the rock this time. Jesus meets her, as he does each of us, at the point of her need.

The Samaritan woman didn't fully understand Jesus, at least not in this brief portrait. I'm not surprised; I don't fully understand either. I cannot wrap the fragile membranes of my mind around divine grace. I cannot conceive of love like living water, flowing much more richly than the deepest well can supply. Indeed, I need this quiet drama simply because of the Samaritan woman's lack of understanding. Then, and perhaps only then, I can take Jesus' words to her as spoken to me also: "Everyone who drinks this water will be thirsty again, but whoever drinks the water I give him will never thirst. Indeed, the water I give him will become in him a spring of water welling up to eternal life" (John 4:13–14). And like her, I, too, can say, "Give me this water, so I'll never thirst again."

There is one more step in this quiet drama of the Samaritan woman and the Living Water. When she asks to drink of that water, she gets more than she ever dreamed. She came to know the source of living water himself. The scene closes, and still the woman's confusion persists. But she has worked earnestly with what she knows to fathom the mystery of eternal life, and she has asked for the Living Water that leads to eternal life. And now her seeking is fulfilled beyond her wildest expectations. "I know," she says, "that Messiah...is coming. When he comes, he will explain everything to us" (John 4:25). Jesus' response buckles one's knees: "I who speak to you am he" (John 4:26). It is one of the first announcements of himself as Lord and Savior of the world, and given in response to a simple request for Living Water.

I stand in awe of this woman. Her faith is stronger and purer than mine. Her audacity makes me look like a coward. But what her quiet story tells me is that the same love and grace flowing like Living Water for her also flow for me from the Messiah.

Psalm 107:35–36

He turned the desert into pools of water
   and the parched ground into flowing springs;
there he brought the hungry to live,
   and they founded a city where they could settle.

Prayer

I come before you like the Samaritan woman,
confused, lacking understanding
of your holiness and your majesty, Lord.
As you did with her,
will you open me to your springs of living water,
that I may drink deeply of eternal life?
Amen.

Day Twenty-Four

THE LIVING WATER: FLOW RIVER, FLOW

The gracious invitation from Jesus to drink from the Living Water is not limited to the Samaritan woman. She stands in our place in this story. Although uncertain and confused, she is given an invitation to drink from the well that will never run dry, and she steps forward. She asks in faith; she receives the spiritual flow of the Holy Spirit.

This is a story of glory and newness. It is a resurrection from a parched spirit to a fresh land. Like maple buds after an April rain, like a dry garden now dancing with daffodil blossoms, life has swollen and burst forth. This is our resurrection story also. We are as much the Samaritan woman as the wondering women at the empty tomb. Glory has sprung forth and flooded the plains of the wasteland.

What particularly strikes me in this story, however, is how real and present Jesus is to this woman. In an incredibly intimate moment, just the two of them by the well, Jesus probes the secrets of her life and lets her open herself. There is much to tell. By any standards she would probably not be judged a "good" woman. She has, in fact, had five husbands, and is currently living adulterously with another man. There is no evidence of any particular piety, no quoting from sacred texts or the law. Very likely, the circumstances of her lifetime have made it more convenient for her to forget than remember.

But all that fades to insignificance in the presence of Jesus. He is here, at this spot and this moment, for *her*. One would almost think that she is the very center of his life, the very reason for his existence at that moment. Indeed, Jesus is. The story overwhelms me because, if I can see so much of myself in the Samaritan woman, then I can also see Jesus before me as he was with her. I, too, am washed clean by the miracle of Jesus meeting me at the well in a dry and thirsty place.

Like learning to swim in a mud puddle, my mind flails at the edges of knowing God. He is at once God above and beyond all things, one of such majesty that to look upon his face was to die, and yet also he is God Immanuel, of such tenderness that he walked among us men, women, and children and wore a crown of thorns that streaked his all-too-human face with blood. The picture slides. One seems to be the God I approach with the rational mind, all the catechisms and texts clutched to my chest as a kind of protection. Before the other I want to bow down and wash his dusty feet with my tears. But, and here's the mystery, they are one and the same—Lord and Savior met in the person of Jesus.

Our knowing God and our discovery of authentic faith lies, like the Samaritan woman, in simply giving up our lives to him. I cannot do it anymore, Lord. It is all yours. I don't understand this earthly situation anymore than I can understand the engineering intricacies of some bridge. But I'll ride on it, and let you support me while I go.

The story of this remarkable woman, however, doesn't end in that dusty little town of Sychar in Samaria. Because Jesus is the Living Water, it extends far beyond that. This is the same God who divided the waters at creation, who parted the sea for the Israelites to cross, who stopped the Jordan at flood stage, who made water burst out of a rock. Does anyone think this mighty flow can be shut up, shut down, dried away?

If they do, they must turn to the last chapter of the Bible, for the story of Scripture *begins* and *ends* with the flow of water (see Genesis 1:1–2 and Revelation 22). In the final chapter of Revelation, after the wars of the Apocalypse, John is at last shown the eternal city and the first thing he sees is the flowing water: "Then the angel showed me the river of the water of life, as clear as crystal, flowing from the throne of God and of the Lamb down the middle of the great street of the city" (22:1–2). Here is the Living Water. It begins to flow in us now when we come to Jesus, name him our Messiah, and drink of the living stream of grace that will never run dry.

Ezekiel 36:25–26

I will sprinkle clean water on you, and you will be clean; I
will cleanse you from all your impurities and from all your
idols. I will give you a new heart and put a new spirit in
you; I will remove from you your heart of stone and give
you a heart of flesh.

Prayer

Revive me, Precious Lord.
As I draw near to you
during these days approaching
your crucifixion and resurrection,
may I again feel your eyes upon me,
your voice reaching out to me,
your grace like a river
flowing within me.
All in the name of Jesus.
Amen.

THE LIVING WATER:
THE LAKE OF LIFE

We were hiking through a valley that wound among the mountains of western North Carolina—my wife and I, my son, and his friend. The map of the valley proved useless. Once we climbed down into it, we entered a maze of flowering rhododendron fourteen feet high. But it was a good place to be lost, despite its name of "Graveyard Fields." The rhododendron layered a rich pink scent over the valley; copses of blue and yellow wildflowers grew by every small rivulet carved into the valley floor. We followed the spaces that opened before us, taking our direction from the sun.

We knew that to the north a river cut through the valley (it was there on the map), and that it fell into a waterfall right about here. We knew that our van was somewhere south. We couldn't get too far lost and weren't particularly concerned if we did. We had been lost on our hikes before, and always found our way back. Some hikes just lasted longer than others.

We heard the river long before we saw it. It had cut its way down to a bed of large, flat-slabbed boulders and a billion smaller stones that glittered like fallen stars. We shucked our shoes and socks first thing, found a comfortable rock to sit on right where the waterfall started, and let our legs dangle up to the knees in the frigid rush of water. We could feel the muscles go numb.

For two boys, however, sitting on a rock was not their idea of adventure. They spotted a fallen tree far upstream and crossed the river on it. They worked their way downstream on the opposite bank. As they did so, they began to spot protruding rocks, and jumped them out into the river. No problem. The river was fast with the whole valley's runoff, but it was shallow. The small spot where we sat was only knee-deep.

What we couldn't see, and didn't know, was that the river, as was typical through these twisted hills and valleys, began a slope toward the waterfall that grew more precipitous by the foot. It wasn't a sudden drop-off at all. As it went faster, it grew shallower, allowing the smaller stones in the riverbed to acquire a silvery mica shine that made them as slippery as ice. My son, ever the daredevil, ever the showman—and quite hot in the sun after our hike—decided to sit down in the middle of the river. He moved slowly at first. It seemed like great fun. He lifted his hands above his head like a roller-coaster ride. Then he was going faster. He careened off a large boulder. We called in horror. It was a hundred yards yet to the thirty-foot waterfall, yet he seemed miles away from us. Miraculously, and I mean that word seriously, he remained sitting up, bouncing off boulders, that blond hair caught in silver spray. Then he disappeared. We began clambering over the shoreline rocks downstream.

At the bottom of the falls was a twenty-foot deep pool. Some college kids were swimming there. How they must have been surprised to see this small body come hurtling through the air. How wonderful that they were there to help him out. When Joel got to the shore and had taken several deep breaths, he gave a large, flamboyant bow.

When we thanked one of the college kids afterward, he said, "It's a miracle he stayed sitting up. It's the only way he could have survived. Two people died going over this falls last year."

Sometimes life and death stand only seconds apart for us in this life. And sometimes they do in eternal life also. The book of John's Revelation portrays two seas that illustrate this. One is the Sea of the Beast—the demon of sin and the antichrist. This is not the first mention of that sea in the Bible. Old Testament prophets looked forward to the day when the Redeemer would slay the "monster of the sea" (Isaiah 27:1). Often in such cases the monster is described as "leviathan" or a "great serpent," much like the Beast of Revelation.

The most stirring prophecy about the sea in the Old Testament occurs in Micah 7:19: "You will again have compassion on us; / you will tread our sins underfoot / and hurl all our iniquities…into the depths of the sea." Clearly our sins are trod underfoot when Jesus crushed the head of the serpent Satan. The beautiful part, however, is that thereby our sins are hurled into the depths of the sea, impossible for us to locate. They are buried.

But, as Lent reminds us, we are not just liberated from our sin—although that is glory enough—but we are also liberated to a joy that is unimaginable to us now. Therefore Revelation draws the picture of two seas. One is the lake of fire where Satan and his allies will twist and burn in eternal agony (see 20:10). They are locked up there. Never again will they touch the lives of the redeemed with sin or suffering.

Then John hears these words, "It is done. I am the Alpha and the Omega, the Beginning and the End. To him who is thirsty I will give to drink without cost from the spring of the water of life" (Revelation 21:6). Yes. We have heard those words before—to the Samaritan woman. John writes that the "angel showed me the river of the water of life, as clear as crystal, flowing from the throne of God and of the Lamb down the middle of the great street of the city" (Revelation 22:1–2). This is the Great Sea of Crystal, flowing throughout all eternity. We drink of it now from the Living Water; we will rejoice in its purity for all eternity. In this city there will be no more night (see Revelation 22:5) for the Lamb is the light. There will no longer be the curse of suffering (see Revelation 22:3) for we will eat of the tree of healing.

There is one very simple way to the blessed city. As Jesus said to the Samaritan woman, the angel says to John: "Whoever is thirsty, let him come; and whoever wishes, let him take the free gift of the water of life" (Revelation 22:17). It is as stunningly simple, and as earthshakingly profound, as that.

Come, drink deeply of the water of life.

Revelation 22:20–21

He who testifies to these things says, "Yes, I am coming soon."

Amen. Come, Lord Jesus.

The grace of the Lord Jesus be with God's people. Amen.

Prayer

Alleluia!
I wish nothing else
and nothing more
than to drink of the Water of Life.
Cleanse me,
nourish me,
refresh me,
renew me, I pray.
Amen.

Day Twenty-Six

THE DOOR: KNOCKING

I was a first-term, first-year deacon. At this particular church the primary task of the deacons was not collecting and distributing funds to the needy. Rather, it was to make the pastoral calls on the shut-ins and other assigned members in our congregation of nearly seven hundred members. Needless to say, my list was quite lengthy. But with the zeal of a new deacon I determined that I would call on every single person on my list during that first year.

I mentioned that to a fellow deacon. He pointed to one name on the list—I'll just call her Mrs. Meilander—and said, "Good luck." On the chart after her name not one call had been made during the past ten years.

Most of my members were shut-ins, in nursing homes and the like. I noticed that they had not been visited often so I started with them—and thoroughly enjoyed it. Some of them I visited several times that first year. But for some reason I waited with Mrs. Meilander. Ten years! What was going on? And she lived only three blocks from my own house.

Finally I worked up the courage one evening, right after the dinner hour. I thought I'd catch her at home. I dressed nicely, practiced a killer of a smile. I walked to her house and rang her doorbell. Nothing happened. Waiting an appropriate minute, I knocked on the door. Again. I was about to try to peer through the lace curtains over the windows alongside the door, when suddenly a narrow little blue-veined hand pulled the curtain aside. Her small periwinkle eyes pierced me. She shook her head vigorously, her tightly pinned gray hair was like a bonnet on her head, and pulled the curtain shut. I stood there for a moment, then retraced my steps home. Maybe I had to practice that smile more, I thought. I am, after all, quite a large man and she was quite a tiny woman.

My next opportunity came after the Easter morning services, when the deacons were given the lilies that decorated the church to deliver to shut-ins. It was nearly a full afternoon's job. Our church had many shut-ins. Why, I wondered, was I saving Mrs. Meilander for last? Of course. She was right on the way home. Only three blocks away.

Again I stood on the porch and knocked. Again I waited. And again, after a long wait, the thin blue hand pulled the lace curtain aside. I held the lily out in front of me so she could see it. A remarkable thing happened then. She cracked the door open, snatched the lily, and darted back inside.

That evening I was lamenting my efforts to my wife. "I'll never get in there!"

Pat looked at me and smiled. "Oh, yes we will."

It took me a few minutes to catch on to her shift in pronoun, from my "I" to her "we."

A few days later the whole family—Pat carrying homemade vegetable soup and cinnamon rolls, I guiding our two toddlers—walked up to Mrs. Meilander's house. The process was the same. But this time, when she pulled the lace curtain aside, something happened in those periwinkle eyes. And, miraculously, the door opened—wide. We all entered her shadowed house.

Perhaps it was a miracle that she opened the door to us. It was surely a miracle that she opened the door of herself and admitted us to her life. That was just the first in what became many visits.

And then this final visit.

We were talking, always now the family and I, in her living room. It was, I was surprised to discover, a restful place. The old furniture was of highest quality and meticulously kept—most of it, I guessed, now collector's items.

"You know," she said, "I'm getting old."

We looked at her expectantly.

"My daughter in Cleveland wants me to come and live with her. I guess I'll go into a rest home there."

"I'm sorry to hear that," Pat said. She, too, had become attached to this strange old recluse who had opened her door to us.

She nodded. "Before I move, I want you to take your pick of my furniture."

We were, of course, stunned. We had just bought our first house, were raising a family, and some of the rooms in the house were pitifully bare of furniture. "I want you to take as much as you want. Whatever you want. I won't need it anymore."

"Mrs. Meilander," Pat said (I was struck dumb), "I really don't think we could do that."

As things turned out, we finally took her mahogany dining room table set. We didn't have one. I'm sure we would never be able to afford mahogany. But it was part of a memory.

That first day I stood knocking on her door, I never expected a gift as priceless as that. I only wanted to get in, to talk with her, to get a bit closer to her. The way was eased by Pat and the children. They opened the door. Once they did, we were surprised to have become friends with Mrs. Meilander, and to receive, eventually, such a gift from her.

This meeting demonstrates one of those unusual and surprising moments of human grace. But suppose for a moment that Mrs. Meilander had come down the street to our house and knocked on the door and said, "I have a gift for you. Not just a table, but a seat at the king's table with a wedding feast spread just for you."

Would you believe it? That's more like Jesus' grace. In Revelation 3:20, Jesus speaks these words to the church in Laodicea: "Here I am! I stand at the door and knock. If anyone hears my voice and opens the door, I will come in and eat with him, and he with me."

Psalm 24:7–8

Lift up your heads, O you gates;
    be lifted up, you ancient doors,
      that the King of glory may come in.
Who is this King of glory?
    The LORD strong and mighty.

Prayer

I cast the doors of my life
wide open, so that the light
of the Son of Righteousness may stream through.
The shadows recoil;
sparks pierce every darkness.
This is the season of joy,
of light and life and your
illimitable love, dear Lord.
Amen.

THE DOOR: OPENING

When I was a young boy—probably around ten—I decided I would make a few bucks selling greeting cards. My eye had been caught by an ad in the back of *Boy's Life,* a magazine I faithfully read whenever my father took me with him to the downtown library. Marvelous prizes accrued to the top salesman too, all the way up to a chrome-fendered, fat-tired, Schwinn bicycle.

I managed to sell my first allotment of cards by dint of sheer determination and a good set of legs that set me trudging up one block after another. Some people passed a few kind words with me. Some shook their head, not a word spoken, and shut the door. Some actually pitied me and scrabbled for some loose change to buy a box of cards. I couldn't blame any of them too much. I thought the cards were hideous. Even with my limited artistic appreciation at age ten, they seemed to me cheap and tacky.

The scene varies altogether for those we await or those who are friends. I know parents who have waited years for a child to come home and knock on the door. They would give anything to hear that knock. And when friends come knocking, who among us would hide in another room with the lights off? It isn't so much that the door opens as it is that our hearts open.

When Job finally made his defense to his tormenting friends, one of his key points was that "[N]o stranger had to spend the night in the street, / for my door was always open to the traveler" (Job 31:32). Who among us can claim as much? Indeed, the unqualified act of mercy and extension of comfort claimed by Job becomes central also to Jesus' teachings. In his lesson on the king's division between the sheep and the goats in Matthew, the king says, "I was a stranger and you invited me in" (25:35). And when the "righteous" inquire about the meaning of this, the king adds, "I tell you the truth, whatever you did for one of the least of these brothers of mine, you did for me" (25:40).

The fact is that we come to heaven's door, which is only and always Jesus himself, as one of the least of these. That's it: we stand stripped of all titles, of all earthly achievements, of all earthly relationships.

Here, however, is his promise of the open door: "Ask and it will be given to you; seek and you will find; knock and the door will be opened to you. For everyone who asks receives; he who seeks finds; and to him who knocks, the door will be opened" (Matthew 7:7–8). This door stands before us not in some vague future sense, but at this present moment. The door of Jesus' death and resurrection stands open before us; we have only to walk through by saying "I believe."

What happens when we walk through that door? I have visited people in their homes and left feeling more of a stranger than when I entered. Not so through Jesus' door. He supplies his answer for us in the Gospel of John. Nearing the conclusion of his intimate conversation with his disciples, Jesus says, "I have told you this so that my joy may be in you and that your joy may be complete. My command is this: Love each other as I have loved you" (15:11–12). Then he adds a spectacular benediction, "You are my friends if you do what I command [that is, love one another]. I no longer call you servants, because a servant does not know his master's business. Instead, I have called you friends, for everything that I have learned from my Father I have made known to you" (15:14–15). When we enter this door of belief in the present, and then the door of eternal life in the future, Jesus awaits us and says, "Welcome, my dear friend." That's his promise.

What else does it mean?

It means that there was a time when we were lost. Now we are found. Now our names are inscribed in the Lamb's Book of Life as Dear Friends.

It means we were once known as sinners. Now we are known as Saints. In his letter to the Colossians, Paul gives thanks to the Father "who has qualified you to share in the inheritance of the saints in the kingdom of light" (1:12). We are saints, "set apart" for a life in Christ.

It means that once we were foreigners. Now we are family. Once we were aliens. Now we have been taken in. Once we were condemned. Now we are approved of and dwell in the fellowship of the forgiven.

All this happens through the door Jesus opened for us at the crucifixion and resurrection. We have only to enter, saying "I believe."

Revelation 5:8–10

And when he had taken [the scroll], the four living creatures and the twenty-four elders fell down before the Lamb. Each one had a harp and they were holding golden bowls full of incense, which are the prayers of the saints. And they sang a new song:
"You are worthy to take the scroll
    and to open its seals,
because you were slain,
    and with your blood you purchased men for God
        from every tribe and language and people and nation.
    You have made them to be a kingdom and priests
        to serve our God,
        and they will reign on the earth."

Prayer

Will you add my prayer of thanks
offered up to the throne of God,
dear Jesus? You have opened
the doorway on faith and fellowship,
on life and love,
and have let me walk through
by the price of your perfect love.
Alleluia! What a Savior.
Amen.

Day Twenty-Eight

THE INTERCESSOR:
OWNING OUR SIN

Recently I attended the memorial service for a man much loved and respected in the community and by his family. I shared those sentiments. Reflecting on all the years I had known him, I could not recall hearing a mean or angry word from him. He was a man born with a smile and a contented heart. So at the memorial service a long train of children and grandchildren stepped forward to testify to his faithfulness and godly life. It was an earthly fanfare for his entrance into glory.

Memorial services invariably invoke in me a peculiar sadness. Most certainly it is a grieving for the particular friend or relative's death, but it seems to go beyond that. I relive the loss of those I have loved; I cherish the presence of those I love who are still living. The liturgy of the service itself cracks the door wide on feelings too long hidden or tucked away in the back reaches of memory.

But this service lingered in my mind for another reason. It turned me inward on myself. Hearing the accolades for this man's seemingly unimpeachable life, I began to wonder what could be said for my own. Finally, I decided, it could only be as simple as this: He has been forgiven.

I have no idea of how eternal matters work, of course. I find the Bible a bit indirect on particulars and differing views confusing. Just for a minute, suspend all the conflicting views and imagine that there really is a gatekeeper at heaven's glory. Or consider, as Scripture gives us greater evidence for believing, that there is an adversary at heaven's throne. Suppose I stand there before this adversarial being who argues against my admission. I don't know what his words of challenge will be, or if he'll even utter any. The words on my behalf will more than suffice: He has been forgiven.

Most importantly, those words will be spoken by the One who has the authority to utter them—simply because he has paid for my forgiveness. If any word is to be spoken against me, he will intercede for me. This Jesus is precisely the one whom Isaiah prophesied in his great Easter message. According to Isaiah, "[H]e bore the sin of many, / and made intercession for the transgressors" (53:12). I am one of those transgressors. I need an intercessor, one who will testify: He is forgiven.

But, forgiveness of *what* exactly?

Perhaps a very few Christians lead such holy and exemplary lives that they feel themselves beyond the need for forgiveness. Or, perhaps they are living the ultimate delusion. Others have lacquered their lives in simple denial; they can't engage any confrontation with their need of forgiveness lest the glossy surfaces shatter. This is a curious situation, because the very essence of our confession of Christianity lies in forgiveness. We need grace. Jesus is the source of forgiveness and grace that restores joy.

Generally, though, we humans fight against self-exposure. We don't like to be seen as messy and weak. We do, on the other hand, like to be seen as capable and self-sufficient. Basically, we like to be seen as successful.

Here the problem arises. If I am self-sufficient, I don't particularly need an intercessor. I am capable; I am successful. I can do it on my own.

Isn't that the jingle of the modern age?

The problem is that it leaves a lot of lonely people in its wake—from the janitor scrubbing the bathroom to the executive in her fourteenth-floor, glass-windowed office. The antidote to the poison of loneliness—the grinding emptiness telling us that despite all the successes, something awfully important is missing—is love. Yet, strangely, we often resist divine love.

I think there are three things to remember here. I'll put them in the first person, because I have experienced them all.

First, I have to admit that I need love. Desperately so. I have grown afraid of spiritual loneliness, and no amount of self-sufficiency can fill it.

Second, I need to learn to receive love. I have to recognize that I do have worth in someone else's eyes, not for what I've done but for who I am. Who I am is this—a child of God. Somehow God thought me worthy enough to have his Son intercede for me.

Third, I need to learn to give love. Love seems to do little good when it's simply received and stored up in a Mason jar in some corner of the heart. It's more like a stream. As I give it away to others, it can keep flowing fresh into me.

Hebrews 7:24–27

…because Jesus lives forever, he has a permanent priesthood. Therefore he is able to save completely those who come to God through him, because he always lives to intercede for them.

Such a high priest meets our need—one who is holy, blameless, pure, set apart from sinners, exalted above the heavens. Unlike the other high priests, he does not need to offer sacrifices day after day, first for his own sins, and then for the sins of the people. He sacrificed for their sins once for all when he offered himself.

Prayer

Lord, during this Lenten season
my thoughts turn uncomfortably inward
upon my own sin
and my need for your interceding grace.
Give me the strength not to "duck out"
of my sins. They are my own.
I admit it. I confess it.
I place myself before your cross
asking for a renewed and right
spirit within me.
Help me start over, Lord.
Amen.

Day Twenty-Nine

THE INTERCESSOR:
OWNING OUR GRACE

Consider this. One of the traits of our modern age may be called *generic grace*. That's grace by our own terms, grace without really confronting the need for it or the source of it.

The very act of forgiveness requires two things. It requests *pardon* for a sin committed and *freedom from* that sin committed. These may seem at first glance identical, but consider that pardon focuses upon the *act*, whereas freedom focuses upon the *doer* of the act. Both, however, require grace for forgiveness.

This again raises the problem of self-confrontation. What was the act committed? Do I accept whole responsibility for that act? Often we try a spiritual short-circuit around both and go directly for the grace. This path is doomed to failure.

As he did so often during times of stress, when his mission on earth seemed to weigh heavily upon him, Jesus retreated to a garden. The Garden of Gethsemane was nothing at all like our conception of modern gardens, with their abundance of colors and fragrances. In fact, it was mostly rocky ground on the lower slopes of the Mount of Olives just outside Jerusalem. Here grew tall, old olive trees, and where old branches fell, the decaying wood nurtured moss and ferns. It was a quiet place, cool in the evening breeze, where Jesus prayed in agony.

One other anguished moment played out there—not of the divine conflict between good and evil that was coming, but one that was all too human. All too much like any one of us.

Peter, all pumped up with his typical bravado, had just sworn that even if everyone else ran away, he never would. "Even if I have to die with you, I will never disown you" (Matthew 26:35). And of all the disciples, we would expect that the boisterous, unruly Peter would go to his death by his Lord's side.

We, too, make such courageous promises. We think sometimes of those brave saints and martyrs who have gone before us and pray for a tenth of their spiritual conviction. But we know the rest of the story of Peter, and too often find our place with him. For at the end, all of his rash promises fail and he too denies the Lord (see Matthew 26:69–75). Perhaps the most haunting verse in the account is the final one: "[H]e went outside and wept bitterly."

Peter understood with a pain deep in his bones that his sin was entirely personal. Only he was culpable. His lips alone spoke the words. He needed grace.

Oddly enough, Matthew's detailed account does not provide the follow-up. For that, one turns to the Gospel of John—"The Gospel of Love and Light." Here James asks Peter point-blank—"Simon son of John, do you truly love me more than these?" (John 21:15). Jesus repeats the question three times, matching Peter's three denials. Each time Peter affirms his love.

Here we have one of the best examples of Jesus' restoring grace in the Bible—he meets Peter at the point of his deepest need and forgives him.

But there is one more step. Each time that Peter affirms his love, Jesus responds: "Feed my lambs." This is our charge also. We are not restored simply for our own sake, but also to nurture those others in need in this world.

Grace flows. The generic grace of our age offers just enough rain to make us realize how dry and cracked the land really is. I need a river of grace.

Romans 8:33–35

Who will bring any charge against those whom God has chosen? It is God who justifies. Who is he that condemns? Christ Jesus, who died—more than that, who was raised to life—is at the right hand of God and is also interceding for us. Who shall separate us from the love of Christ? Shall trouble or hardship or persecution or famine or nakedness or danger or sword?

Prayer

Even though I may at times
feel apart, lonely, and unsettled
in this world, Lord,
I never feel apart from you.
You have promised to be with me always,
even to the end of the age.
And you sealed your promise
with the anguish of grace
so I may glory in it.
I love you, Lord.
Amen.

Day Thirty

THE BLESSING

I t might seem a bit irreverent to speak of one's favorite passage in Scripture. "The Book," as one of my friends calls it, is, after all, a seamless whole, from the birth of light in the first verse of Genesis to the kingdom of light in the last verses of Revelation. Nonetheless, every believer, I suspect, has favorite passages that speak in profoundly personal and meaningful ways. For me, that passage occurs in chapters 14 to 17 of John's Gospel.

It is a deeply intimate setting. Jesus gathers with his disciples, away from the maddening crowd. He calls them "his children," and speaks as a loving father. Knowing what is to come, Jesus first speaks words of comfort to his children: "Do not let your hearts be troubled. Trust in God; trust also in me" (John 14:1). He reminds me of a parent tucking a fretful child into bed at night with words of comfort.

Furthermore, Jesus gives promises: "I will ask the Father, and he will give you another Counselor to be with you forever—the Spirit of Truth" (John 14:16–17). The Holy Spirit will be with us forever, from the second we're conceived to the second we enter heaven. With that promise, Jesus adds, "Peace I leave with you; my peace I give you. I do not give as the world gives. Do not let your hearts be troubled and do not be afraid" (John 14:27).

Jesus speaks words of comfort. He promises the enduring presence of the Holy Spirit. Then he emphasizes his inseparability from his followers by the lovely analogy of the vine and the branches. We derive our very lives from the life of that central vine. His grace flows through our ingrafted veins. Our task as fellow branches, now filled and flowing with the great love Jesus has for us, is to bear fruits of love for others. In fact, Jesus specifies it as his commandment (see John 15:17), just as he did during his Sermon on the Mount. This is a commandment with promise, for the fruit of branches grafted in love is joy: "I have told you this so that my joy may be in you and that your joy may be complete" (John 15:11).

This blessing whiplashes me into reflection in its dramatic power. What other religion is predicated on the promise of joy? Which promises a Holy Spirit to guide believers in love that leads to joy? Truly, many religions make claims to such. But how many deliver? The answer lies in John 15:13: "Greater love has no one than this, that he lay down his life for his friends." There's the miracle no other religion can claim. None at all. "God so loved the world that he gave his one and only Son, that whoever believes in him shall not perish but have eternal life" (John 3:16). This is our joy, as it was of the disciples. It transcends grief, as Jesus says, because no one can take it away: "Now is your time of grief, but I will see you again and you will rejoice, and no one will take away your joy" (John 16:22).

Threaded throughout these passages, moreover, lies another powerful blessing: that God hears and responds to our prayers. Jesus himself intercedes with the father on our behalf (see Romans 8:26). Here we may let the powerful words of Jesus speak on their own authority: "I will do whatever you ask in my name, so that the Son may bring glory to the Father. You may ask me for anything in my name, and I will do it" (John 14:13–14). Again, a few chapters later in the Gospel of John, Jesus emphasizes his promise: "Until now you have not asked for anything in my name. Ask and you will receive, and your joy will be complete" (16:24).

Soon after this tender and emotional scene, overflowing with love and blessings, Judas appears with soldiers bearing torches, lanterns, and weapons (see John 18:2–3). The moment of peace has ended, but the promises never die. In its most basic form, that is true because Jesus not only gives the blessing, he *is* The Blessing. In him, all his promises and blessings are true and unending. From the quiet place he is led away into the noise, the darkness, the confrontation with agony on Golgotha. But, true to his promise, he rose again on the third day and is now seated at the right hand of the Father—victorious, interceding for us.

2 Corinthians 1:20

For no matter how many promises God has made, they are "Yes" in Christ. And so through him the "Amen" is spoken by us to the glory of God.

Prayer

Like the heavenly choir in Revelation
I give blessing and honor and glory
to you, O Lord.
You have given me blessings
beyond measure, because you are Blessing itself.
Unworthy of such, I nonetheless
join that chorus of the redeemed,
and glorify your name.
Amen.

Day Thirty-One

THE RESURRECTION
AND THE LIFE

S
everal years ago a group of people dubbed "The Jesus Scholars"
set themselves the task of determining which sayings of Jesus
recorded in Scripture he actually spoke, or which sayings were
falsely attributed to him. They were serious. Using such tools as lin-
guistic, historical, and social studies, they methodically whittled away
at those red-lettered words in the Bible. Consider one of the losses.

Shortly before the Passion Week, Jesus' earthly ministry was at its
apex. He stayed on the eastern side of the Jordan River, right at the place
where John the Baptist had been preaching a few years earlier. At that
place many came to believe in Jesus. None of his words are recorded;
the fact is simply stated—the crowds came and many believed. It was
the calm before the storm.

What turned the calm was the death of Lazarus, brother of Jesus'
beloved friends Mary and Martha. When the sisters sent word to Jesus
that Lazarus was dying, he did not immediately leap up and rush off
to be with them. Why not? He loved them, surely. But Jesus stayed in
the peaceful region two more days.

Jesus knew, of course, what awaited him in Judea. Peace would
be broken by swords and whips. Jeering would rupture his teaching.
Certainly, this is what the disciples focused on: "'But Rabbi,' they said,
'a short while ago the Jews tried to stone you, and yet you are going
back there?'" (John 11:8). One can't blame them for their nervousness.
Danger awaited in Judea.

Jesus, however, saw beyond the swords and jeers. He saw beyond

Lazarus' dying. By the time Jesus arrived, Lazarus had been dead four days and now lay entombed. Beyond his friend's dying, Jesus saw true life.

Interestingly, in this miracle Jesus provides a lesson for his disciples directly related to the coming cross—which they do not quite see at the time. Jesus' own time on earth steadily narrows to that inevitable encounter with the cross. To the disciples he says, "Lazarus is dead, and for your sake I am glad I was not there, so that you may believe" (John 11:14–15). Believe what? Those disciples must have been mystified, shaking their heads as they traveled along to Bethany. Jesus gives his answer to Martha when he tells her Lazarus shall rise again. No, not on the last day, as she responds. Right now, right here, through Jesus. And so he speaks these words, the very words that "The Jesus Scholars" claim that Jesus would not, could not, have spoken: "I am the resurrection and the life. He who believes in me will live, even though he dies; and whoever lives and believes in me will never die. Do you believe this?" (John 11:25–26). Cut out those words, and we cut out the heart of Christianity. Of course, they're red-letter highlighted in Scripture. Jesus asks each of us, "Do you believe this?"

Our response, if we truly believe, is as simple as Martha's. "Yes, Lord...I believe that you are the Christ, the Son of God, who was to come into the world" (John 11:27). Jesus is the resurrection and the life.

But Martha still doesn't fully comprehend it. Nor do the disciples and watching Jews. Especially not when Jesus tells them to roll away the stone from the tomb. In a loud voice, Jesus calls Lazarus forth from the dead, and Lazarus walks from the tomb. Now perhaps they see. Jesus is the resurrection and the life.

Here also lies the monumental irony, for there were also "Jesus Scholars" all around at his time. Seeing the life-bringing power, they sought to kill the one who defeated death. Indeed, they even made plans to kill Lazarus. In a sense, it is the height of the ridiculous.

Jesus had just raised Lazarus from the dead; now they want to kill them both. No man could do, nor should do, these things. It was impossible and had to be struck from their histories.

Lazarus would have to die eventually, of course. So would Jesus. He would do so as the resurrection and the life for all those who come with the simple faith of Martha.

This was to be the end of Jesus' public ministry. Perhaps he was gathering strength for what was to come, for six days before the Passover, he returned to Bethany, staying at the house of Mary, Martha, and Lazarus. Soon he would head into Jerusalem. The Jewish leaders wouldn't have to plot to kill him after all. He had come to lay his life down. As the resurrection and the life in and of himself, no one could take his life unless he willingly laid it down.

John 3:13–15

"No one has ever gone into heaven except the one who came from heaven—the Son of Man. Just as Moses lifted up the snake in the desert, so the Son of Man must be lifted up, that everyone who believes in him may have eternal life."

Prayer

I see you now, lifted up
on the cross that I may have life.
I see you now, high and lifted up,
in life everlasting,
so that I may live forever with you.
Alleluia! You, Jesus,
are the Resurrection and the Life.
Amen.

Day Thirty-Two

THE MESSIAH

The triumphal entry of Jesus into Jerusalem on Palm Sunday seems to me to be curiously intertwined with the birth of Jesus. There is a cosmic inevitability to both scenes. Mary rode a donkey to give birth to Jesus in a stable. Jesus rode a donkey into Jerusalem to give his life. In the town of Bethlehem, just a few miles south of Jerusalem, crowds thronged about Mary and Joseph as they looked for a place to stay. As Jesus rode from Bethany to Jerusalem, crowds shouted about him, waving branches, throwing their cloaks in his path. At his birth, only a few knew that Jesus had come as the Messiah—God's redeemer. On Palm Sunday, the chanting crowds believed he came as the Messiah—the new political ruler.

What interesting paradoxes. Many had forgotten the true purpose for Jesus coming into the world as Messiah. Many now celebrated their own ideal of his coming. Is it any wonder that, as he approached Jerusalem, Jesus wept? Jesus says, through his tears, "If you, even you, had only known on this day what would bring you peace—but now it is hidden from your eyes" (Luke 19:42). The people had turned from what Jesus had to give them to what they wanted.

And what did this true Messiah truly have to give? That Christmas message itself helps us understand the weeping Savior on Palm Sunday. The story of Jesus' incarnation, the story J. I. Packer calls "Love to the uttermost for unlovely men," is the fulfillment of God's persistent mercy toward his people.

It is little wonder that the Christian world looks forward to the celebration of Christmas with excitement. In the same way, Old Testament

Israelites looked forward to the Messiah's coming. The problem was that they already had defined to the Giver the gift they wanted; their Messiah conformed to *their* shopping list. When the real Messiah appeared, they didn't even recognize him.

Their blindness was not for a lack of adequate signs. Over and over, God sent signs and wonders directing people to the One who was to come. The voices of the prophets seem to rise in agonized chorus. Isaiah cried out, "Hear, you deaf; / look, you blind, and see!" (42:18). The signs were all about. The prophecies abundantly pointed to a coming Savior.

But nowhere, perhaps, is the foreshadowing more powerful than in the characters of Abraham and Isaac. One often wonders whether the grim scene enacted on Moriah is only a test of Abraham's faith, or whether it is a wondrous sign from God to his people—a sign that shows God's intervening grace and his willingness to bear the sacrificial burden. The episode in Genesis 22 would seem to be a startling testimony to the latter.

God calls Abraham to take his *only* son to Moriah, a journey of three days. In a sense, the death of Isaac is certain on the first day, the day of departure. On the third day, at Moriah, Isaac is lifted from the sentence of death. Abraham is called by faith alone; only by absolute obedience to the word of God can he see this grim trial through. Yet Abraham believes; he goes forth. Like Jesus on Palm Sunday, he goes forth to the darkness.

When they arrive at Moriah, the aged Abraham is forced by his infirmity to lay the wood for the sacrificial offering on the back of Isaac. This lamb, too, had to bear the full burden of the sacrifice, just as that later Lamb would bear his own cross on the way to Golgotha.

Still Abraham goes forth in obedience and in faith. One imagines he experiences terrible dread, for he loves Isaac deeply. But he loves God more. As they ascend the mountain, Abraham has only this to say to Isaac: "God himself will provide the lamb for the burnt offering, my son" (Genesis 22:8). What more can he say? He holds the fire and the knife!

Did Abraham know what was to come? Could he know that God's angel would intervene in the split second before the downward plunge of his knife? Of course not. But he believed; he had faith. In what? That God would provide, surely. But this passage, with its emphasis in the original Hebrew, says, "God will provide *himself!*"

Here is the great foreshadowing, for God himself bore our burden on the cross—God in the person of *his* dearly beloved Son Jesus. Abraham left the place, giving it a name of the promise that pointed to the Messiah—the Lord will provide—since "On the mountain of the LORD it will be provided" (Genesis 22:14).

This the Messiah did. He is God's provision for all mankind, longing for the greatest Christmas gift of all. On Palm Sunday he prepared it for us.

1 John 4:9–10

This is how God showed his love among us: He sent his one and only Son into the world that we might live through him. This is love: not that we loved God, but that he loved us and sent his Son as an atoning sacrifice for our sins.

Prayer

Lord, thank you for your ride into Jerusalem,
so lonely even in the throng of adoration.
They sought a king.
You were King of kings.
You knew exactly where this journey led,
and all that rested upon it.
No wonder you wept, Lord.
Was it for me also?
Amen.

Day Thirty-Three

SON OF GOD— SON OF MAN

After a careful study of the New Testament, no one can doubt Jesus' claim to divinity. Among the first to pay homage to him as the Son of God were the demons. In the synagogue at Capernaum, a man possessed by a demon cried out, "Ha! What do you want with us, Jesus of Nazareth? Have you come to destroy us? I know who you are—the Holy One of God!" (Luke 4:34). Later, the two Gadarene demoniacs shouted, "What do you want with us, Son of God?" (Matthew 8:29). And during his temptation of Jesus in the wilderness, Satan, the father of demons, openly referred to Jesus as the Son of God (see Matthew 4:3, 5–6).

There are other times, of course, when Jesus' divine nature is made clear. For example, the Holy Spirit announces Jesus' divinity at his baptism (see Luke 3:22). When Jesus walked on water to Peter, Peter exclaimed, "Truly, you are the Son of God" (Matthew 14:33). Jesus himself spoke of doing his Father's will (see John 6:38–40). That Jesus is the Son of God is the overwhelming theme of other New Testament books as well.

And well it should be, for this is the heart of Christianity: The Son of God became flesh and dwelt among us (see John 1:14). For us, this is an unfathomable truth. Why should one give up the glories of heaven to live as a man and to die like a criminal—worse, to die for crimes not his?

But reverse the perspective. For the Son of God, the truly remarkable thing must have been to become man. Thus, it is not surprising that

Jesus names himself over and over as the Son of Man. The title is used more than fifty times in the gospels. Outside of the gospels, which, of course, concern themselves with the life of Jesus, the name is used only a few times. One of those times is in the Acts of the Apostles, where Stephen says, "I see...the Son of Man standing at the right hand of God" (7:56). But Jesus calls himself the Son of Man repeatedly, reinforcing another marvelous truth: The Messiah, the Son of God, is fully man.

Why the title *Son of Man*? Precisely because all that Jesus does and all that he means is present in *himself*, in his bodily form. In fact, Jesus uses the title when he is making some of his greatest claims for himself.

As the Son of Man, Jesus is the *redeemer*: "For the Son of man came to seek and to save the lost" (Luke 19:10). And also, "For the Son of man also came not to be served but to serve, and to give his life as a ransom for many" (Mark 10:45, *RSV*). Here we might think of a much earlier Old Testament use of the title "Son of Man." In a vision one night, Daniel saw the Ancient of Days, a designation for the everlasting God, take his throne in the heavens. Thousands of angels attend him at the Ancient of Days and sits in judgment.

Then, Daniel writes, "In my vision at night I looked, and there before me was one like a son of man, coming with the clouds of heaven" (7:13). In Daniel's vision, this person was "Like *a* son of man"—indeterminate and indistinct. With Jesus' birth, he is *the* Son of Man. But exactly like Daniel's vision, he comes to establish the everlasting kingdom of the redeemed: "He was given authority, glory and sovereign power; all peoples, nations and men of every language worshiped him. His dominion is an everlasting dominion that will not pass away, and his kingdom is one that will never be destroyed" (7:14).

As Son of Man, furthermore, Jesus is *resurrected* from the dead, having paved a way redeemed people may follow. To Martha, Jesus said, "I am the resurrection and the life; he who believes in me, though he die, yet shall he live, and whoever lives and believes in me shall never die" (John 11:25–26, *RSV*). When Daniel wrote of the "everlasting dominion" (7:14), he had no knowledge of how it would come about, but it was purchased by the Son of Man.

As Son of Man, Jesus *ascended* and prepared a place for those who will be resurrected to be with him: "I tell you, hereafter you will see the Son of Man seated at the right hand of Power, and coming on the clouds of heaven" (Matthew 26:64, *RSV*). This is a stunning promise. We, too, will meet the Son of Man in all his resurrected glory.

Finally, as Son of Man, Jesus will *return again:* "For the Son of Man is to come with his angels in the glory of his Father, and then he will repay every man for what he has done" (Matthew 16:27, *RSV*). This, Jesus says, will be "the renewal of all things" (Matthew 19:28). We, too, shall be renewed at his return.

None of these events would be possible unless Jesus became the Son of Man. The true glory lies here: The Son of God became Son of Man to redeem the lost, to resurrect the redeemed, to ascend and prepare a place in glory, and to return again to judge the world.

Romans 5:17 (RSV)

> If, because of one man's trespass, death reigned through that one man, how much more will those who receive the abundance of grace and the free gift of righteousness reign in life through the one man Jesus Christ.

Prayer

> Dearest Savior,
> I pray that in all the routine events
> of each day that passes here on earth,
> and during those events when we wish
> that the days might pass more quickly,
> I will be mindful that you came
> as the Son of Man,
> That you arose from the dead,
> That you have prepared a place for me,
> where I will dwell eternally
> with you when you come again.
> *Amen.*

A QUIET PLACE

We had been anticipating this event for six months. I and several close friends who meet weekly in a Bible study group had made reservations for a weekend retreat at an abbey in southwestern Michigan. It took weeks for us to coordinate openings on our calendars with that of the abbey. When the day came, it couldn't have seemed like more of a disaster.

We left work early that day on a highway raked by thunderstorms. Earlier in the day tornado warning sirens had blared through the sultry air. Lightning lashed out of black clouds; rain savaged the windshield. The others rode together in one car, but I had to leave late in my ten-year-old compact car. That little car bucked in the wind like a beach ball. Any time I went above 60 MPH, it seemed to be lifting off into flight. In the first forty miles there were three traffic jams. A tractor-trailer had jackknifed across the highway and two cars had slid into spins off the road. Then things got really bad.

A van pulled up alongside me, the driver blowing the horn and making the universal down-pointing hand signal that strikes fear in the heart of any driver. With a sinking feeling I angled off the expressway, as far away from the sucking roar of the semi as I could. I stepped out and watched the left front tire collapse as I stood there. Usually I pack a tool kit, gloves, and my old Army jacket when I travel out of town; this time they were all in my wife's van, our usual "travel car." Well, I would have to see what I could do, as cleanly as I could do it. Then it was that I noticed that suddenly, inexplicably, the onslaught of rain had stopped. I raced to the trunk, got out the jack, and began spinning that thing like it was a hamster on an exercise wheel. I had the tire off and that silly little Mighty Mouse of a spare on within five minutes. As I slammed the trunk, hands blotched with grease and grime, the clouds opened and the rain came down like it was held up for too long. I sat there inside my car a few minutes, wiping my hands as best I could on some backseat litter, my heart slowing to a steady thud. I wondered about my panic, my desperation, only moments before. I gave thanks.

Then I looked in the car manual to see how fast I could travel on that thing that looked like a bicycle tire on my front wheel. Dinner was to be served at the abbey at 6:00 PM sharp. The handbook said 50 MPH for the spare. I figured I'd go for 55.

I arrived at 6:30, finding my way down the long, winding road by headlamps that barely pierced the darkness and lightning that flooded the sky. Oh, was I happy to arrive. Except that I learned that dinner was served at 6:00 PM. On the dot. If you're not there, you don't eat. And breakfast, we had heard, was a small bowl of cereal and a piece of fruit. Very well, I'd fast. It wouldn't be the first time and I thought an abbey retreat an appropriate time. I put out of my thoughts the fact that I hadn't eaten since 11:00 AM.

After the anxiety of the traveling and during the constant rumbling of the storm, it took awhile to settle down. But an eerie sense of peace seemed to emanate from the very walls that protected us. My friends, who had by now grown worried, rejoiced with me. During a lull in the pounding rain, we rushed to the chapel for compline and let the slow chants and songs of that special hour hold us. We returned to our individual rooms for prayer, but then we just sat together in the common room, talking, relishing the peace of being able to do that without having to look at a watch.

Quiet came as we made space for it.

Finding a quiet place is at once the easiest and the hardest task in the world. Prying ourselves out of the torrid pace of our lives sometimes seems a virtually impossible effort. So many demands seize our time, squeeze it hard, and throw it away. It was so for Jesus. During his triumphal entry of this Passion week, he needed a quiet place—the upper room—to be with his disciples. Even into this quiet place, however, his ancient foe entered and smiled his hideous deceit. There would be no more quiet for Jesus. The shouts, the night fires, the jeering were just the beginning.

In Job 26, the tormented Job declares to his friends that we are just too puny to know all of God's greatness. Job describes the power of creation as God's revelation, but also says that "these are but the outer fringe of his works" (26:14). Our knowing doesn't reach far enough to understand God. But God's love comes close enough to embrace us. Here indeed is the radical mystery of the Christian faith. How do we know this embrace of love, then? As with Elijah (see 1 Kings 19:12), it comes in a whisper that we can hear from our quiet place.

This must be added. A day will come, as the Revelation of John tells us, when that voice will thunder and the foundations of the earth shall shake. Out of his mouth a sharp sword shall issue forth to strike down the nations. At the sound of that voice, every knee shall bow and every tongue confess that Jesus is Lord.

And we who have met him in a quiet place will be foremost in the choir singing praise to that king.

Psalm 23:1–3a

The LORD is my shepherd, I shall not be in want.
  He makes me lie down in green pastures,
he leads me beside quiet waters,
  he restores my soul.

Prayer

I wonder what it was like
in that upper room with you, Lord.
This was the last quiet place for you
on this earth, alone with the friends
whom you loved, and the one who
was about to betray you.
Love and pain stood side my side.
Lord, speak to me, I pray,
as I quietly make space for you,
knowing that because of the pain
you suffered, there is now
only love between us.
My heart is a quiet place, waiting for you.
Amen.

Day Thirty-Five

RECEIVING
THE GIFT OF QUIET

The primary thing we seek during the Lenten season is to draw close to Jesus and know him as Lord. That is why we meditate on who he is, how he has revealed himself to us, and why he did this for us. We want to receive the gift of his love, open it, and treasure it.

We draw apart in order to draw close. The world clangs around us like cymbals and drums out of rhythm. We have to remember that it is *you* Jesus loves—not the things you do or have done, but you.

I was trying to understand this miracle of Jesus' deeply personal love when I turned to my journal and found there an entry for the next morning at Saint Gregory's Abbey. Although long forgotten, it taught me once again about the gift of quiet and the gift of love.

> *We have just celebrated the Eucharist here at Saint Gregory's Abbey, but it is only now, as I sit on a small wrought iron bench in the early morning sun, that its meaning becomes clear at the heart level. We can partake of the sacrament so often and in so many new ways, yet at the heart it is always one way and one place: the way a person enters communion with Christ and becomes one with him. So it is that after the act, I must seek the solitude of letting the act become an action in my heart.*
>
> *It is quiet now. Instead of the musty echoes and shadows of the abbey chapel, morning sun sifts through leaves already turning toward autumn. We, my friends and I, drove here yesterday through*

a world torn apart with thunderstorms. Shafts of lightning sliced a sky gone dark by 2:00 PM. Last night, as I fell asleep, thunder growled across the fields outside my window. This morning it is so very still.

One of my friends saw a flock of wild turkeys late yesterday during a break in the storm. Now I can hear them gobbling in the cornfield some distance away, their sounds faint and plaintive. So still. The only other sound is the light breeze drying the leaves. It is the stillness where one becomes one with the Savior.

The sunlight brings out all kinds of delicate colors on the landscape. The mowed fields bear flecks of red and fuchsia like an Impressionist painting. The forest path is gaudy with the bright orange flash of a sumac crawling upward along the base of a tree. On the abbey grounds, where I now sit, the inner court is a temple of oaks, their bases thick with age, bark scarred and peeled loose at places (lightning?). It is a wonder that the spreading hostas survived the storms yesterday. Perhaps the oaks protected them, for here they are, their delicate white and lavender flowers waving gently like votive candles in the breeze.

On all the circular brick walkways of the courtyard, edging into the beds of hosta and myrtle, damp fields of moss spread in random patterns. But over all, the quiet beauty. It is the beauty where one begins to sense the beauty of the Savior—an action ongoing rather than a one-time act.

Stillness of the heart. Beauty to the spirit. Yet there is this thing—objects for the mind to contemplate. They are random and varied as if placed by whimsy rather than design. Benches rest here and there, as if begging one to come and be still. A sculpture, about seven feet tall and in the mode of Giacometti, points its stiletto shape heavenward. In a far part of the courtyard rests a strangely shaped, pagoda-like structure. It rests heavily upon the earth. And, oddly, at different points are old, rusted water pumps. When were they used? Who used them?

I drove home that afternoon under a Michigan sky, the light big and the blue as keen as forever. The far north, seen only from the crest of farm-swept hills, held a handful of fleeting cirrus clouds. Behind me one of my friends followed closely. We traveled slowly, below the speed limit that I soon forgot about. Cars passed and ceased to exist.

God was as much present in the crash of the storm as in the quiet, windless blue of the present. We found each other in quiet withdrawal. The cloister walls of the abbey were merely the "accident" of our meeting. It could be any place, at any time.

I had been alone with the One who is never Alone, never separated from me.

We were present in the presence of each other.

1 Timothy 2:5–6

> For there is one God and one mediator between God and
> men, the man Christ Jesus, who gave himself as a ransom
> for all men.

Prayer

> Jesus, Sod of God and Son of Man,
> Thank you for coming close to me.
> Give me strength to walk by your side,
> in your way,
> and in your path.
> Quiet my heart
> so that I many hear
> your voice leading me.
> *Amen.*

Day Thirty-Six

LAMB OF GOD: THE COVENANT

A minister friend once observed to me, "The bottom line of Christianity is the shedding of blood."

My mind recoiled. No! The bottom line of Christianity is grace, or forgiveness, or peace. But then I reflected a few minutes. How do all these qualities, which seem the cornerstone of our Christian faith, come about? As it should, the statement of my friend drove me back to the Bible.

Immediately I thought of the many expressions of Jesus as the Lamb of God in the Book of Revelation. They are as stunning as they are puzzling. In the fourth chapter, John sees the door of heaven open in his vision. The sight is spectacular, far beyond the imagination of some Hollywood techno-wizard. Rainbows lace the throne room; lightning flashes, and thunder rumbles. Throughout, celestial creatures raise a hymn of praise to Almighty God. Then a scroll appears in the hand of the one seated on the throne, and an angel calls out, "Who is worthy to break the seals and open the scroll?" (Revelation 5:2). In this cataclysm of divine power, John weeps, until an angel tells him that the Lion of Judah—that great Messianic title from Genesis 49:8–10—has come. But a lion doesn't come. Rather, a Lamb does. And more—a lamb that looks like it has been slain.

Revelation might well be called the Book of the Lamb. It tells the triumph story of the one who was slain, who now rules in heaven, and who is coming again. Yet the mystery remains. Why? How did this rule come to be, and why was the crucifixion absolutely necessary as the cornerstone or Christianity? We shy away from bloodshed. It is a sign of danger to us, of life leaking away. We want to stop the leakage at all costs before more damage is done. How, then, can we possibly rejoice in the slaying of the Lamb of God? To understand the mystery, we have to turn back the pages of biblical history practically to the beginning of time itself.

In the Old Testament times, the lamb was one of the most common sacrificial animals. This would not be unusual. Many of the Israelites were herdsmen, and sheep had the unique ability to eke out a life on the often desolate and arid landscapes of Judea. The sheepherders led them out to the hills, found their watering holes, protected them against prey. Sheep were, one might say, a central part of the people's life. From them they took wool for clothing and blankets, meat for their food, milk for consumption, their skins for leather, and their sacrificial offering. Special conditions attended the sacrificial lamb. It could not just be some old, sickly creature, destined to die in the hills, nor some scrawny, underdeveloped animal. It had to be a lamb of a year old, and one altogether without defect (see Numbers 6:12–14). In short, the lamb had to be the very best to serve as the offering.

But why must it be offered at all? We might quickly think of sin atonement—the guilt offering. Something precedes that in the story of the lamb, however. It began with the first bloodshed in human history. After that jealous and hot-tempered man Cain slew his brother Abel, God said to him (and one wonders what the tone of his voice was), "What have you done? Listen! Your brother's blood cries out to me from the ground" (Genesis 4:10). Carrying the life of the person, that blood also carries the image of God in that person. The shedding of blood is so grievous because it destroys the possibilities God has for that person. Psalm 72 puts it like this—God "will rescue [the needy] from oppression and violence, / for precious is their blood in his sight" (72:14). And that preciousness with which God holds us is why the first offering of the lamb's blood appeared as a covenant.

That covenant becomes clear when the Israelites were about to flee from Egypt. Paradoxically, the covenant of the lamb comes on the very night when, because of their willful ignoring of the Israelites' need and the brutal shedding of the Israelites' blood, the Egyptians' own cruelty will come to rest upon them. Always in Scripture the pattern appears that cruelty and willful bloodshed will exact a price. But the Israelites will be, on this terrible night, secured under a seal of protection. Each was to offer a small lamb and sprinkle its blood on the doorposts and lintel of their homes. These homes, and these only, would the angel of the Lord pass over. Therein lies the covenant of grace, sealed by the blood of the Lamb.

The sacrifice of the lamb as a sin offering during the following Old Testament history is a natural extension of this covenantal act. The sin offering brings the blood of the lamb in our place—representative of our sins, offers it up to God, and relies on his covenantal grace for forgiveness. The picture is incomplete, however, if we consider it as a rite of some long-distant past, only vestiges of which stay alive for us in those difficult books of Old Testament law. Step back a moment and look at the larger picture.

Religion as we know it begins when a people respond to their God, and for Christianity that is precisely the moment when Adam and Eve responded to God's voice in Eden. Into the rapture of this pristine world, in which each moment was perfect worship, slipped the voice of sin, wrecking the world like a gouging monster. It feasted on the life God created, and took its most diabolical turn when Cain destroyed the life of God's supreme creation—humanity itself.

The shedding of blood was sin, and sin cut humanity off from God. The only way of drawing close to God again was the atonement offering of sin. The lamb intervened. It took the place of sinful humanity and through God's restorative covenant was accepted by grace. But this atonement offering was an act repeated over and over. As the weight of sin pressed down on this fallen world, there could never be lambs enough. Or could there? Could there be a lamb of the world?

Could there be a Lamb of God, come to take away the sins of the world?

John 1:29

The next day John saw Jesus coming toward him and said, "Look, the Lamb of God, who takes away the sin of the world!"

Prayer

Oh, Lamb of God, dear Lamb of God,
precious is your blood that flowed.
It washed me of my sin
and restored me to your side.
I'm tired of being separated,
alone in my gray sin world.
My only offering is myself
on the altar of your grace.
Amen.

Day Thirty-Seven

THE SACRIFICE

Smudge pots fill the early morning air with their acrid smoke. It is still cold as the half-light of dawn filters into the Roman square. You know about this part of town. It is a place to be avoided. You watch from the shadows.

Then they drag him out, roughly. He has eaten little since the Passover meal several days before. He has wept and prayed in the garden, endured a shuttling between higher-ups who haven't quite known what to do with him. He has broken no laws in their books, but somehow he is a dangerous man. Too dangerous. His own people want him dead. The higher-ups solve their problem. They turn him over to his own people for judgment. Death.

Now the sun falls into the square. The squad of Roman soldiers—this will be done in an orderly fashion, after all—bind him to the scourging post. It is a distasteful job, hardly one for the elite. Some of the squad are drunk. They spit on him. They beat him on the head with clubs. They mock him as they tear off his garments and tie him to the scourging post. From where you kneel in the shadows, feeling your stomach rebel, you hear the cracking snap of the scourging whip.

He is so weak now he cannot bear the cross up the hill of Golgotha. You think once again of running away. Even the drunken mockers are starting to find other things to do. But the Roman squadron—the death squad—enlist a young, muscular man to carry the cross. Things must go on. Get it over and done with.

But they have no accounting for what happens. Nor do you as you huddle on the far side of the hill, hidden by brush and rock.

As the sun nears its noonday zenith, a film settles over it. It seems that its very light turns away, fading to gray, then a thick darkness. It is cold now on the hill. The wind swirls eddies of dust across the knob and you can scarcely see the three rude crosses poking scarecrow-like into the murk. You hear voices—women's voices weeping, words from the figure sagging on the cross. He utters one last, echoing shout: "*Eli, Eli, la'ma su bach-thá ni?*"

You think the darkness will never end; it is as thorough and thick as fear. You kneel rooted to the spot, too terrified to run. Then, suddenly, the darkness begins to lift, like some miasma being sucked away. But as it does, the ground itself begins to tremble, as if the darkness were being sucked out of the deepest bowels of the earth. It feels like warfare between earth beneath and heaven above, the darkness wrenching and twisting loose. Rocks shatter under the force. It's hard to breathe.

The soldiers want to have it done, to flee this place. They have to finish their job. That's what they're here for—this death squad. To finish them off. And so one man hurries to the middle figure—quickly now!—and thrusts his sword into the man's side. The sword penetrates lungs and aorta cavity. Blood and fluids gush out.

He is already dead. He has yielded up his spirit.

This is the sacrifice of the lamb.

The Lamb of God.

The lamb who is God.

He has laid down his life for his sheep (see John 10:15). Jesus has redefined the "Good Shepherd," as he has redefined the sacrificial lamb. Only he has enacted the work of each, at once, and for always. No more does the blood have to splash the altar as we grasp desperately for grace. No more do we have to search for a shepherd who is "good" enough to lay down his life for us. Those final words from the cross roll down through all the years since: "It is finished" (John 19:30). Turning to Jesus, we turn also into his sheepfold of which he has said, "My sheep listen to my voice; I know them, and they follow me. I give them eternal life, and they shall never perish; no one can snatch them out of my hand" (John 10:27–28).

Flick your mind a moment back over that wind-ridden rock called Golgotha. There was nothing pretty about this place when the darkness ate up the sun. Only horror. Remember how you trembled from afar at the ugliness of it all. Out of *that* came our peace. Only if the words of the Lamb are true—"I lay down my life for the sheep." But the glory is that the deed is finished; we now walk under the care of the Good Shepherd, whose love will never let us go.

Revelation 5:12

> In a loud voice they sang:
>> "Worthy is the Lamb, who was slain,
>> to receive power and wealth and wisdom and strength
>> and honor and glory and praise!"

Prayer

> Do I deserve your sacrifice, O Lord?
> The thought scares me.
> Precisely because I don't deserve it,
> I claim it, and hold onto it
> with all the strength I can find.
> You are my Lamb of God.
> Honor and glory and praise be to you,
> now and forevermore.
> *Amen.*

Day Thirty-Eight

SOME CALL HIM LORD

In the last, painful moments of Jesus' life on this earth, there were few to witness his dying. In the darkness crouched the faithful women who had attended and loved him. Perhaps one or two of his disciples hidden in the dark. A squadron of Roman soldiers. And, of course, and closest to him in his dying hours, hung two others on their cross of pain. They were thieves, those who stole from people, and ironically flanking the one who was giving his very life for people.

Then, while the people and one of the thieves mocked Jesus—it continued to the very end—the other thief pleaded, "Jesus, remember me when you come into your kingdom" (Luke 23:42). He had, spiritually, come to the altar; he affirmed his need for Jesus; he begged for eternal life through the precise event that was being enacted on the cross not a dozen feet away. The sacrificial lamb was being slain.

The truly stunning words were from Jesus, "I tell you the truth, today you will be with me in paradise" (Luke 23:43). Jesus always and only told the truth. *Today* you will be with me in paradise. With the offering of the lamb death itself is crushed. This deed enabled Paul to say, in echoing the words of the prophets Isaiah and Hosea: "Death has been swallowed up in victory. / Where, O death is your victory? / Where, O death, is your sting?" (1 Corinthians 15:54–55).

Often, however, I find myself back at the altar. Like the thief, I whisper in the darkness, "Jesus, remember me." I need the reassurance that he promised me, "This day you will be with me in paradise." That is my altar now, enacted during the darkness and solitary suffering of my Savior. I come with no offering other than my need.

It takes an act of infinite courage to cleanse the altar of our hearts, to make our very lives—heart, soul, mind, and strength—a sacred place for God. But it is always the first thing. Before we even think about building our public temples, we need to purify our personal altars.

Sometimes this can be a lonely and fearful process. One might well say, I am really, really afraid to open myself up like this. I feel so exposed, so...messy and weak.

Consider the latter comment first. Of course, one feels exposed, messy, and weak at the altar. That is why we come. None of us is alone in that. Paul writes in Romans 3:23–24, "[F]or all have sinned and fall short of the glory of God, and are justified freely by his grace through the redemption that came by Christ Jesus." We come precisely because we are weak. We can't make it on our own.

Consider the other hesitation, this matter of fear that one has coming to the altar. I think we all, individually, have fears before the altar where we meet God. We fear that we are not worthy, that the altar will remain vacant and lifeless, that our offering will be scorned. I know I have.

At the altar you are alone with God, and to him you are of infinite worth. The most amazing thing is that, unlike any other religion in the world, you don't have to earn your worth before coming to the altar. It is earned by the coming itself, for the altar is our meeting with the perfect sacrifice, Jesus. We lay our unworthiness on the altar. That is all we have to offer. We walk away loved and held by the Lord who bestows worth.

Way back in 1566, some spiritual leaders got their heads together to define the essentials of the Christian faith. Although there are points of disagreement among denominations about this Heidelberg Catechism, all Christians find unity in the ringing truths of the first question and answer. You can see what I mean.

> Q. WHAT IS YOUR ONLY COMFORT IN LIFE AND IN DEATH?
> A. That I am not my own, but belong—body and soul, in life and in death—to my faithful Savior Jesus Christ.

He has paid full for all my sins with his precious blood, and has set me free from the tyranny of the devil. He also watches over in such a way that not a hair can fall from my head without the will of my Father in heaven; in fact, all things must work together for my salvation.

Because I belong to Him, Christ, by his Holy Spirit, assures me of eternal life and makes me whole-heartedly willing and ready from now on to live for him.

To fully appreciate this answer, look at the verbs. They remind us of all the things Jesus has done for us:

He has *fully paid…*

He has *set me free…*

He *watches over me…*

He *assures me of eternal life…*

Like the thief on the cross, I come to the altar, and call him—Lord.

Hebrews 13:15

Through Jesus, therefore, let us continually offer to God a sacrifice of praise—the fruit of lips that confess his name.

Prayer

Lord, accept the praise of my lips,
and the thanksgiving of my heart,
before the altar of your loving sacrifice.
Amen.

Day Thirty-Nine

WOMAN, WHY ARE YOU WEEPING?

Tinges of frost lie in the garden. Shadows tremble in the predawn light. But it is quiet, quiet and, oh, so lonely. Yet she comes with the shadows.

She is beyond fear. Nothing can touch her, because she has already seen the worst happen. She has watched her Lord die, and this is where they placed him.

She leans against the rocky wall. Inside—inside lies his body. As dawn forms the eastern sky, she leans there, weeping. She thought she had no tears left. But, because of the long Sabbath, she has not been able to come here to mourn. Tears splash her cheeks like a veil.

Oh, Mary, why are you weeping?

She edges around the rocky face of the tomb. Something is wrong. Something is terribly wrong. One hand against the rock, steadying herself, she creeps forward. She pauses to rub her eyes clear. The new light of the sun does not lie. The stone, that great stone that covered her Lord's tomb, had been moved. What could this mean?

Mary runs, bearing news and looking for answers, to Simon Peter and John, two of the leading disciples. Her voice is frantic, shrill—"They have taken the Lord out of the tomb, and we don't know where they have put him!" (John 20:2). Grave robbers? The Jewish authorities? Surely not the Romans! But this—how can you come to a place to mourn, and there is no body there? No wonder Mary is weeping. She has lost her Lord *twice*.

Then the interesting things begin to happen. Peter and John race to the tomb and stumble over the facts: the tomb is empty; the burial linens are flung askew, as if shaken off; the cloth that bound Jesus' head lies neatly folded nearby. John steps inside the tomb. Empty, all right. Bewildered by it all, they wander back home.

Mary stays, this brave Mary the Magdalene. She stays, weeping. Suddenly she is aware of two bright, white-clad figures sitting in the tomb, one at the foot, the other at the head of where Jesus himself had lain. In her sorrow, Mary probably doesn't see the significance we do—the heavenly bright angels represent victory over the darkness of death.

Then an interesting sequence of events happens. How does weeping turn to joy? Follow Mary's Easter experience a bit further.

First the angels ask her, "Woman, why are you weeping?" (John 20:13, *RSV*). Notice that they speak first to her need, her distress. Mary is weeping.

Once more Mary says, "They have taken my Lord away...and I don't know where they have put him" (John 20:13). There lies the distress. Jesus' body is gone. Mary, still weeping, turns around. She sees a man standing there—a live man, not a dead one. Of course, she doesn't recognize him. She expects to find death, not life. She thinks he is the gardener.

The man's words echo the angels': "Woman, why are you [weeping]? Who is it you are looking for?" (20:15). Mary's offer to the presumed gardener is astonishing: "Sir, if you have carried him away, tell me where you have put him, and I will get him" (20:15). Mary thinks to put Jesus in his proper place—the tomb. She will honor him by placing him where he most definitely belongs.

But Jesus no longer belongs in the tomb. With great tenderness, he simply speaks her name—"Mary." And she sees, and she knows. How her heart must have leapt: her Lost is found, he is alive.

Mary runs to the disciples and exclaims: "I have seen the Lord!" (John 20:18).

It started in the frosty darkness as Mary came to mourn the dead Lord. But now everything made sense. Everything he said came true. Remember? Mary did. And at that moment, without further questions and having all her answers met by Jesus standing before her, her heart danced with joy.

The increasing joy of Easter is that Jesus still stands before us, each one of us individually, calling our name. Mary, John, Patricia, Daniel, why are you weeping? Look up. See, I am here, alive. Death could not hold me; sorrow could not defeat me. I bring to you the boundless joy of everlasting life.

John 20:29

Then Jesus told him [Thomas], "Because you have seen me, you have believed, blessed are those who have not seen and yet have believed."

Prayer

Gracious Savior,
Thank you for your powerful revelation
to Mary that turned her sorrow into joy.
Thank you for your Easter resurrection
which makes all things new.
Amen.

Day Forty

THE FAITHFUL AND TRUE: RESURRECTION SUNDAY

To be called "faithful and true" in the Hebrew nation bore special significance. The Israelites were a warrior people, dwelling among other warrior people. The land was unsettled politically, frequently ablaze with military campaigns as armies battled for their land and the protection of their people. In spite of the warlike conditions of nations, and in spite of the Israelites' frequent wanderings among them, we are surprised to learn that they had no regular standing army until the reign of King Saul. At a time when nations depended so heavily on military strength, this seems odd indeed. One could no more imagine the modern United States without its armed forces.

The fact of the matter is that before the reign of Saul the Israelites as a whole were a military power. Each able-bodied man was held accountable to answer the call to arms. The leader, usually one noted for past heroic deeds, issued the call for battle and every man who was faithful and true answered that call. Only newlyweds and cowards were legally exempted. The leader needed men he could count on, those faithful to his call and who would be true to his cause.

No military can operate otherwise. Many of us who are veterans would probably like to forget those grueling weeks of basic training, but this we remember: the training was as much psychological as physical. Intensive strategies and programs trained us to be faithful and true.

It is, perhaps, a sad commentary on our time that we need training to be faithful and true. For the Israelites, the call was made by the leader and the people responded. Yet, we live in a different time, an age of such thundering change that we sometimes wonder if anything can be faithful and true. Few of us indeed have escaped deception and falsehood, sometimes from those whom we love most. The longing for stability sometimes issues as a plea that seems to stick in our throats. Whom can we depend on?

Like the Old Testament Israelites as a warrior nation, the name Faithful and True is given to Jesus as the conquering leader. To be sure, the adjective *faithful* is frequently used to describe Jesus' teaching. He is the one who had overcome Satan and thus bears the surety of our salvation. He is the one we can depend on.

This image of Jesus as the conquering leader, however, emerges dramatically in Revelation 19. The great warfare with the Beast and with Babylon, the worldly city, has exploded across the face of the earth. A hideous warfare it is. The harlot Babylon has enticed great kingdoms into slavery to her. They have bowed down to her in their lust for power and wealth. Babylon's own power resided in the ageless menace of the Beast, the one who "was, and is not, and is to ascend from the bottomless pit" (17:8, *RSV*). The terrifying fury of the apocalypse unleashes across the scarred face of the earth as the warriors of darkness and the kingdoms, represented by the multiple heads of the beast, assault the Lamb of God.

This is a scene to buckle the knees. The nightmare of all ages emerges incarnate. But—and with Jesus there is always that significant *but*—the power of the Lamb and those with him called the "chosen and faithful" reign victorious. No creature of the created order can be superior to the Creator. The Lamb is the Lord of lords and King of kings.

As the cataclysmic fury subsides, as the Beast and Babylon are subdued, a great shout arises in heaven. "Hallelujah" crescendos above the diminishing roar. The great "Praise God" fills the earth. With thunderous praise the heavens crack open and, riding a white horse, comes the Faithful and True. Indeed, he is faithful to his promises. Indeed, he is true to his word. And he has conquered.

The badge of his conquering is there for all to see. His glistening robe is "dipped in blood" (Revelation 19:13). Whose blood? His own. The very blood by which the Lamb bought the victory, the purchase of salvation. He has already paid the price to defeat the beast. So it is that this one, who is called the Faithful and True in the pattern of the Old Testament leader-hero, leads his army, now clad not in the dirty fatigues of battle, but in the victory apparel of fine, white linen, and riding upon white horses in the victory procession.

Now, and forever, the Lamb is Faithful and True.

Today is Resurrection Sunday. All the battles have been fought. The Lamb has conquered, even the last enemy—death. Now he leads us in life, on a great white horse, the Faithful and True.

Psalm 89:1

I will sing of the LORD's great love, forever;
   with my mouth I will make your
      faithfulness known through all generations.

Prayer

What matchless love is this, dear Jesus,
ever faithful, ever true?
In this world of change
and the furious swirl.
I pray that I will be
ever faithful to you.
Amen.